ACTING OUT

MERIDIAN

Crossing Aesthetics

Werner Hamacher

Editor

Translated by David Barison, Daniel Ross,
and Patrick Crogan

*Stanford
University
Press*

———

*Stanford
California*
2009

ACTING OUT

Bernard Stiegler

Stanford University Press
Stanford, California

How I Became a Philosopher was originally published in French in 2003 under
the title *Passer à l'acte* © 2003 Éditions Galilée; *To Love, to Love Me, to Love Us*
was originally published in French in 2003 under the title *Aimer, s'aimer, nous
aimer: Du 11 septembre au 21 avril* © 2003 Éditions Galilée.

Printed in the United States of America on acid-free, archival-quality paper

Library of Congress Cataloging-in-Publication Data

Stiegler, Bernard.
[Passer à l'acte. English]
Acting out / Bernard Stiegler ; translated by
David Barison, Daniel Ross, and Patrick Crogan.
p.   cm.—(Meridian, crossing aesthetics)
"How I Became a Philosopher was originally published in French in 2003
under the title Passer à l'acte; To love, to love me, to love us was originally
published in French in 2003 under the title Aimer, s'aimer, nous aimer."
Includes bibliographical references and index.
ISBN 978-0-8047-5868-0 (cloth : alk. paper)
ISBN 978-0-8047-5869-7 (pbk. : alk. paper)
1. Philosophy, French—20th century.   2. Individuation (Philosophy)
3. Narcissism.   I. Barison, David.   II. Ross, Daniel, 1970–
III. Crogan, Patrick.   IV. Stiegler, Bernard. Aimer,
s'aimer, nous aimer. English.   V. Title.
VI. Title: Aimer, s'aimer, nous aimer.
VII. Series: Meridian (Stanford, Calif.)
B2430.S752S7413 2009
194—dc22
2008006687

Contents

How I Became a Philosopher

The intimacy and secret of my life

"How does one become a philosopher in the intimacy and secret of one's life?"

This is the question Marianne Alphant addressed to me,[1] and to others, and with it she thrust me (and it was doubtless the same for the others) into an embarrassing position. And in reflecting on it I told myself that, in its *après-coup*, becoming-a-philosopher appeared to me in effect and precisely *as* the *secret* and *intimacy* of my life, in the strict sense of these words.

Philosophy and vocation

Becoming-a-philosopher, I first asked myself: is this a vocation and, if so, does it apply to me?

Vocation, according to its original religious meaning, is a name "given to those who 'feel called,'" writes Catherine Clément: "*Vocare*, to call, signifies that all vocations are addressed to the individual, called by his name, as himself."[2]

Religious vocation *is therefore individual.* It *happens* to the individual: it is a *moment* of that which I am about to call a *process of individuation.*

As for extending the religious sense of vocation to profane pursuits, it designates less the event of a call than the existence of a *gift*. One thus speaks of the vocations of musicians, of writers, of artists who *devote* their life to a special *gift*—in the sense of being something rare.

In the *philosophical* vocation—if such a thing exists—there does not seem to be this dimension of *specialty*: no one is devoted to philosophy in particular; *all* of us could be *devoted* to philosophy, which would immediately constitute *a gift, precisely, common to all*. The philosophical vocation cannot be a determination of such and such individual in particular. *All of us*, precisely insofar as we form a *we*, would be devoted *in potential* to philosophy, in a way that is not the case for other kinds of knowing. And, reciprocally, though we know certain people are gifted in poetry, drawing, or music, it seems more difficult to say that someone "has a gift for philosophy."

If there are people *more particularly "devoted"* to philosophy, this would be, then, insofar as they are capable of *making the passage to the act* from a common potential.

This is the first reason why I gave to this lecture, which I dedicate to the memory of Gérard Granel, the title *Passer à l'acte*. Because it is *here* that the *individuality* of the vocation is marked: in the *singularity* of the passage to the act of a common gift, the philosopher would, like a monk, essentially be the individual singularity of a *name*. But how could this *happen*? If it is as a calling, *from who or from what* would such a calling come? And from what circumstances would such a call come to pass and "pass to the act," if it does not issue from a special gift?

Philosophizing through acting

For philosophy, more than for any other profane activity, one tends to understand vocation in a religious sense, insofar as philosophy *through acting*, as the call of a task, should always be, in the whole of its being, and through all the points of its existence, in *accord* with its philosophical "vocation," right down to the "intimacy and secret" of its existence, even *as* this intimacy and this secret.

In fact, this inscription of the philosophical at the heart of the very intimacy of the individual is what is testified to by the life and by the death of that proto-philosopher Socrates—with that sacrificial dimension which is undoubtedly part of an existence completely devoted to thought. The singularity of Socrates' existence, his individuality, was precisely Anytus' accusation, before the trial that would condemn him.

But this inscription of the philosophical at the heart of individuality only makes sense insofar as it is *indissociably and exemplarily tied* to the destiny of this *other individuality that constitutes the City*: this is what Socrates testifies to and in a way *institutes* in the course of his trial and during the weeks between the pronouncement of the verdict and his execution—as reported in *Apology, Crito,* and *Phaedo.*

I believe that in order to more closely consider the incommensurable inaugural impact of the philosophical individuality of Socrates, model of all philosophical existence, we must today appeal to the concept of *psychic and collective individuation,* as forged by Gilbert Simondon. The *existential* dimension of *all* philosophy, without which philosophy would lose all *credit* and sink into scholastic chatter, must be analyzed through the question of the relation of the *I* and the *we,* in which consists this psychic and collective individuation.

I *and* we *in the process of individuation*

That man, as Aristotle says, is a political animal means that I am not human except insofar as I belong to a social group. This sociality is the framework of a becoming: the group, and the individual in that group, never cease to seek out their path. This search *constitutes* human time. And if the time of the *I* is certainly not the time of the *we,* it takes place within the time of the *we,* which is itself conditioned by the time of the *Is* of which it is composed. What Simondon calls *individuation intimately* ties together these two dimensions of the temporality of the political animal.

Individuation is not individualization. Individualization is the *result* of individuation, which is itself a *process*, through which diversity in general, that diversity *which I am* and equally the diversity *which we are, tends* to unify and, through that, tends towards the *in-divisibility* of the in-dividual, that is, its pure *adequation* to itself. Now, the *I* can only individuate itself through its contribution to the individuation of the group that says *we*, that is, to the *cohesion* of that group: this is, *firstly*, what Simondon's concept teaches and formalizes. *But, secondly*, it teaches that the tendency toward in-dividuation is asymptotic: I *tend* to become in-divisible, but I never quite get there. I tend to become *myself*, as indivisible, as pure unity, identity, but I never cease to contradict myself because, in myself, individuating myself in the group that individuates itself through me, I never cease to find myself *other than myself*, I never cease to find myself *divided*, while at the same time the group *alters* and *divides itself*—and it does this because a process of individuation is *structurally incapable of completion*.

From out of this double constraint comes the temporality of individuation. In effect, if every *I* is inscribed in the *we* that constitutes it, and that it constitutes, if the *I* and the *we* are *two faces of the same process of individuation*, at the core of which develops their *tendency* to become-indivisible, ceaselessly projecting their accomplished *unity*, this projection is never concretized except *by default* [par défaut], in other words by ceaselessly *deferring* this completion which, if *realized*, would be the *end* of the process of individuation or, in other words, the end of the individual. Having become himself, completed, no longer changing, a finished individual, achieved, he would be without future. The *end* is, then, since it can never be *realized*, ceaselessly *fictioned*. This is true of the psychic individual that is the *I* just as much as[3] it is of the collective individual that is the *we*.

It is insofar as they are *structurally incomplete* and thus *fictioned* that the *I* and *we* are temporal—and this is why they constitute *histories* in the course of which things come to pass and events *happen*.

The *I* and the *we* are two phases of the one process, in the first place because they share the same preindividual funds, which constitute a transindividual horizon.

> Participation [in the social], for the individual, is *the fact of being an element in a much vaster individuation*, through the intermediary of the stock of *preindividual reality that the individual contains*, that is, thanks to the potentials it harbors.[4]

At the very moment I speak to you, I am in the process of individuating myself: individuating myself means seeking to constitute the symbolic coherence of my utterances. But I will only succeed in individuating myself *if I succeed in making you individuate yourselves with me*. If my individuation succeeds, it will have to have succeeded *in you*—but not at all in the same manner, because what I am in the course of telling you I understand and interpret as some thing *that you understand as some OTHER thing*, and this is what is interesting. This is the *condition of the we*, and it is what develops "potentials," *powers*, or, in Greek, *dunameis*.

However, in individuating the *we together*, you and I separately, and also you and I insofar as we form a group, we participate as well in the individuation of *that which ties us*: language, philosophy, law, etcetera, that which constitutes for us a preindividual fund.

The nonknowledge of individuation and the beginning of philosophizing through acting

It is within the framework of such a process that, in all his activities, Socrates participates in the individuation of the City, and, right up until the end, and therefore *to the extreme*, he links his individual destiny to collective destiny: right up to his death, *which is at the same time the end of his individuation and the beginning of the* we *that is philosophy*. Socrates, by *tying his death* to the City in a certain manner, *inaugurates* the philosophical attitude that necessarily founds all philosophy, as an exemplary relation of the *I* and the *we*. Now, this end is also, therefore, an *infinitization*.

When Crito proposes that he escape, Socrates refuses, because if he did, he says, his children would become orphans—Socrates' children are the City's children, before they are Socrates' children. It is better they become orphans of Socrates than of their own city.[5] And this is why, he goes on, either it is necessary "to bring the city around [to my point of view] by persuasion, or to do what it commands," upholding its laws without reserve, as it were "in life and in death." So, this *death* has the *legacy* of an *obligation*: that of *continuing to interpret* the laws of the City *beyond* the death of Socrates, just as much as *from* that death, a death that becomes also a kind of survival, a *kleos*, a posterity—even if not, as Plato will incorrectly try to demonstrate, an immortality.

In that regard, Socrates' death *remains* incomplete—charged with "potentials." This is his genius.

In contrast to science, philosophy is always the philosophy of *a* philosopher, and, as Nietzsche said, the first question posed by the philosopher is "who?" This means that at the end of the day, *philosophy as the discourse of the philosopher is always par excellence the discourse of an individuation that*, insofar as it is *always at the same time* individuation of an *I* and individuation of a *we, unfolds within its OWN PARTICULAR LIMITS*, through the existential singularity of a philosophical individuality, and precisely as *unachievable*.

Now, this means it is impossible to *constatively* objectify what individuation is. It is impossible to "know" individuation, writes Simondon, without *pursuing* this individuation, without *transforming* it, *for example in inaugurating thereby a new attitude, which is philosophy through acting*.

> We cannot, in the habitual sense of the term, know individuation; we can only individuate, individuate ourselves, and individuate in a we; this seizing is thus at the margins of knowledge, properly speaking.

This is why Socrates' thought is a nonknowledge. But this also means that the discourse of individuation is *performative* (in Austin's sense):[6] philosophical *saying* is necessarily *also* a *doing, to the death*, and this *theoria* is always also a *praxis*—failing which it is nothing but chatter. The question of philosophy is first of all that of *action*.

As a consequence of this question of the articulation of the *I* and the *we* of the philosophers, a philosophical life ought to be exemplary: the philosophy of a philosopher only makes sense when it is illustrated through his way of life—that is, of dying. To articulate his existence and his thought in a manner such that they don't contradict each other: this is a particular experience of the *impossible*, even though it is also of the *truth*, and as a *truth of the impossible*. It is an experience not only of mathematical, physical, artistic truth, but of the truth as such: a way of living, if not in the truth (which would evidently be an illusion), at least in the *question* of the truth, in the *call* or ordeal of the truth such that it is not reducible to any particular activity, which thus constitutes what Blanchot will call "the question of the whole."

Now, straightaway—this is also the beginning of the history of philosophy, and the whole *individual* history of a philosopher— the question of the *truth* is that of the truth *of the origin*, the question of the *true* origin, which exposes itself for the first time, in its *properly* philosophical form, in *Meno*, as the question of the origin *of virtue* and of its *exemplarity*, which is, precisely, what links the *I* and the *we*.

The question of the origin and the desire for knowledge

The question of the origin is what constitutes the whole of human individuation, that is, the whole of *desire*: the whole of human being insofar as it is *essentially* desiring. So philosophy is essentially, at least at its beginning, a search for the origin, and it is in this sense that one could say that every human being is philosophizing—insofar as it is always and from the beginning *unsettled* about its origin. This is what Blanchot says in reference to Freud:

> Freud more or less says that all the questions impulsively posed by children serve as relays for the one they do not pose, which is the

question of the origin. In the same way, we interrogate ourselves about everything, in order to sustain and advance the passion of the question, but all questions are directed toward one question alone—the central question, or the question of the whole.[7]

The question of the origin is immediately an erotic or libidinal question: it is, *literally speaking*, the question *of* desire—the question *posed by* desire, which does not cease to question, and the question *that poses itself* from the moment when one questions desire, when one asks of desire what it is. In *Symposium* Plato has Diotima say that knowledge is by nature radically erotic, and that this is why philosophy is the love of knowledge but insofar as *knowledge is essentially a lack*—just as every object of desire is a lack.

Desire is always desire for knowledge precisely in the sense in which I have posited that *humanity, as a desiring being, is always potentially philosophizing*.

And from that point of view, *I* do not think of myself as having *personally* a particular philosophical vocation: I think I have the vocation the whole world has for philosophy. I think, and I have always thought, that I am devoted as we all are to philosophy, as we all are insofar as we *are*. But the question would nevertheless also be, and this is a noticeable shift, to know if we are not thus devoted insofar as we *become*. Such is the meaning of the question of *becoming-a-philosopher posed from temporality understood as the process of individuation*, and this itself as the passage to the act of a potential philosophical vocation common to all the *I*s that form the *we* which we are and which we become.

The passage to the act as transgression

The question of philosophy *in potential* is that of the *passage to the act* of philosophy.

This is so, even though *passer à l'acte* is also a psychoanalytic expression. It designates, in the course of treatment, a failure where, says Freud, "instead of remembering" (in the therapeutic framework of the transfer of desire), the analysand acts out. This action can designate suicide (and Xenophon describes the death of Socrates as a kind of suicide) but also, more generally, one form or another of *transgression.*

Now, we will see that there is also, when it comes to philosophy, on the one hand a *neutralization of action,* which it is tempting to assimilate to the operation of a transfer of desire—permitting the overcoming of a blockage that is a kind of neurotic dimension *of the City*—by a methodical and passionate practice of *logos* (as dialectic) through which the potential philosopher becomes an actual philosopher. And, on the other hand, *the passage to the act of philosophy* would have a relation to limits, a radical experience of limits of which the first name (but not the only one, nor the last) would be "origin." And, with that, this passage to the act would have a relation to individuation, as already mentioned—being taken in its *political* sense, and as a *vocation for transgression,* in a certain way *to the limits of the law,* of which Socrates will be the index and the protophilosophical infinitization, indefinitely interpretable.

So, this passage to the act of philosophy as politics, where philosophical performativity founds *saying* as *doing,* leads us also to Marx's words, according to which it is necessary to pursue the *interpretation* of *being* through its *transformation*—in *becoming.*

Reminiscence

I have not always been philosophizing "through acting"—if I ever have: up to the age of twenty-six I had not *ever* philosophized; I did not even finish high school. One day, nevertheless, this vocation common to all the beings we are in potential, and in which consists all self-interrogation of the origin, revealed itself almost as a *necessity*—a necessity *literally inevitable and inescapable.*

At the origin of philosophy, with Plato, the *question of the origin* opens itself as the *question of reminiscence.* Now, the question of the origin was also and first of all presented to me *as* this question of the origin, essentially through a *recollection,* which then became the properly philosophical *question* of reminiscence, of Platonic *anamnesis.*

When Marianne Alphant proposed to me that I speak of the intimate and secret way in which I became a philosopher, I was extremely uncomfortable, not only because in itself the question is enormous, but also because this way was constituted through a very singular intimacy, and *precisely* as a secret—all of which took place by accident, which is what still holds me back from speaking of myself in terms of a philosophical "vocation," but this also concerns the whole of philosophy, because I came to place the accident *at the very heart* of philosophy, and perhaps as its unsolvable secret.

Marianne Alphant's question put me back (beginning October 10, 2002, when I commenced reflecting on it) in a philosophical posture in which it is not easy to remain, which one has a tendency, in everyday life, to *forget,* and this was precisely the posture of reminiscence—beyond simple recollection. This question concerning the intimacy of my becoming-a-philosopher led me to a return to myself, plunged me back into moments that I had, if not effaced from memory, at least forced into the background of my existence, even though these moments concerned an origin: the origin of my passage to the philosophical act, but which inscribed itself in another genre of passage to the act.

Reminiscence was at the origin of my entry to philosophy, in such a way as to be essentially tied to a *very existential* experience of reminiscence, which only came to me as it led me into the philosophical attitude, quite by accident, and it is that of which I have had a *second reminiscence,* of a kind, on the occasion of this reflection on the intimacy of my becoming-a-philosopher that brought me today before you.

The necessity of telling the truth

When, for the first time, they appeared to me as such, the questions of origin and reminiscence presented themselves to me immediately as the question of the *truth.* In fact, the question *of the origin* is the question of the *truth* of the origin, and as such it is immediately the question of *truth itself.* Reflecting on the opportunity to respond to Marianne Alphant's invitation, I decided to turn and squarely confront this question of the truth, such as I *encountered* it at a moment in my life in an almost palpable way, as if it had a body, literally as if I could grab hold of it, as one says. Of course I have in fact never really touched it. But *it* has certainly touched me, in one way or another.

The question having been suddenly posed to me of my philosophical "vocation," inasmuch as such a vocation exists, it got me thinking that it *was time* that I reconstitute, through an anamnesis, the question of the truth in the way that, precisely, it constituted itself for me as the question of the *truth of time*—it was time that I again posed the question, and that I exposed myself to it, as it had accidentally proposed itself. It seemed to me it was my *duty*, in a certain way (and it is a heavy word, of which I nevertheless bear the weight), it was my duty to *say*, if not the truth, at least the *necessity* of telling the truth, and in the attempt, as far as possible, to get to the bottom of "my truth," the truth of my journey through the question of the truth and, perhaps, as *the experience of the impossibility of telling the truth other than by default, as the fiction of an après-coup: in time and as time, as the work of time.*

Philosophizing by accident

My becoming-a-philosopher through acting, if it has taken place, and *I believe* indeed it has taken place, was the effect of an anamnesis produced by an objective situation in the accidental course of my existence. The accident consisted in five years of incarceration, which I spent in the Saint-Michel Prison in Toulouse, then in the Muret Detention Center, between 1978 and 1983—years obviously preceded by a passage to the act, that is, by a transgression.

So, these were five years spent in philosophical *practice*, in *experimental* phenomenology, and in passage to the limits of phenomenology, following this "passage to the act" that itself had absolutely nothing to do with philosophy.

One must always be ready to philosophize *to the death*, as did Socrates, and to philosophize *in that dying* which a life is—but "a life" means here an existence and a facticity, an accidentality. For example, Socrates' being condemned to death is an accident that is *necessary*. Socrates will *make sure* that it is necessary, he will make *a mistake that he will have had to make*. The philosophical vocation, if there is one, gives itself, as in Proust, in the future anterior of an *après-coup*, as endurance of the *après-coup*.

The *après-coup* traverses and structures what those five years in prison were for me—but also the following twenty years, which have led me today before you as *before the law*, years I have consecrated to consolidating this "necessity," this mistake that will have had to happen.

But, at the same time, this question of vocation is that of a vocation by default, or by accident, because this vocation is *always that of everyone*, with "everyone" forming the *we* that the philosopher through acting represents in individuating—by default.

Like a flying fish

My incarceration in Saint Michel Prison, result of a passage to the act, will have been the suspension of my acts and the interruption of my actions: such is the function of prison. But *interruption* and *suspension*, which are also the beginning of philosophy (Socrates' *daimon* is the one who interrupts), were for myself the *occasion* of a reflection on what *the passage to the act is in general*—and a recollection of *all the acts that brought me there*.

Twenty years after my liberation, it seems to me, moreover, that my journey will never cease to be a circuit between "action" and its suspension by "philosophy in action" [*"philosophie en acte"*], between writing and highly social activity.

It would be necessary here to examine the ambiguities of the relation between these words, *act* and *action*, with all the problems posed by the translation into the Latin *actus* of the Greek *energeia*.

It is Aristotle who forms this couple of *act* and *potential* with which I have tried on this very day to think my own life—but which I discovered almost twenty-five years ago, in Hegel's *History of Philosophy*, where he reformulates, in his commentary on *On the Soul*, the Aristotelian question of *dunamis* and *energeia* as the question of the *in-itself* and the *for-itself*.

In that treatise Aristotle poses three types of souls, according to three modes of animation, three kinds of living *movement*: the vegetative, sensory, and intellective souls, which form three relations to the "immovable prime mover," to God as the desirable par excellence, as the *motive* and in that sense the *reason* of everything that moves. Aristotle explains that a *sensory* soul, for example, is most of the time sensory in potential and not in acting. It is sensory through acting only when it *reproduces itself*. The rest of the time, it remains in the *inferior* mode of the vegetative soul, which Aristotle also calls *nutritive*. The same applies to the intellective or noetic soul: it is only rarely in action and remains most of the time in the sensory mode. It is in action only when, participating in the divine, it *re-produces* the *truth*. This is what leads Hegel to say that the sensory soul is the *in-itself* of the intellective soul and, in a way, its material. The intellective soul is most of the time only in potentiality, and not in action, meaning that it comports itself sensitively rather than intellectively.

This account, and the lesson it names, will have guided all my solitary work, since the time of my imprisonment—the question becoming that of the *conditions* of the passage from potential to act, *what Aristotle names participation in the divine*. In this regard, reading *On the Soul* was decisive for thinking movement, motion, and what one might call emotion as desire, that is, the relation to the immovable prime mover, insofar as, for such a *passage from potential to act*, the consideration of *milieu* appeared to me to be decisive.

Studying the senses, Aristotle underlines in effect that one does not see that, in the case of touching, it is the body that forms the milieu, whereas, for example, in the case of sight, the milieu is what he calls the *diaphane*. And he specifies that this milieu, because it is *that which is most close*, is that which is *structurally forgotten*, just as water is for a fish. The milieu is *forgotten*, because it effaces itself before that to which it *gives place*. There is always already a milieu, but this fact escapes us in the same way that "aquatic animals," as Aristotle says, "do not notice that one wet body touches another wet body" (423ab): water is what the fish *always* sees; it is what it *never* sees. Or, as Plato too says in the *Timaeus*, if the world was made of gold, gold would be the sole being that would never be seen—it would not be a being, but the inapparent *being of that being*, appearing only in the *occurrence* of a being, *by default*.

Aristotle does not in this treatise examine the *noetic milieu* (the intellective milieu), giving place to *logos* (he does this, on the other hand, in the *Analytics*: such is his *logic*). Reading Aristotle, it is this same possibility of the existence of such a noetic milieu, as the *element* of the everyday life of the intellective soul, on which I meditated a great deal in my cell, where I was *like a fish out of water*. There ought to be a milieu of the intellective soul, I thought, just as the senses of the sensory soul have their milieus.

Now, it appeared to me that this milieu was that of language. I set myself to reading Saussure and Wittgenstein. Later the milieu became for me that of the artifact, of the supplement in general, of which language (through which is produced the everyday experience of *logos*) would be one dimension, but of which technical artifacts (consisting of *things*) would form another dimension.

From then on, philosophy consisted of considering the milieu while being able to extract oneself from it, in the same way as a flying fish can leave the water: intermittently. In this extraction, or abstraction, the milieu is brought into view, which is to say, also, *here, taken hold of*, and *like a wall, by default*, as the condition of passage from the potential of the intellective soul to its act, to its *for itself*. From then on, I could not claim that I was in my cell like a fish in water, but, *in that cell*, where I had been rendered radically deficient in the *vital milieu of the intellective soul*, the *world*, as the *framework of artifacts forming relations sustaining social relations*, I had perhaps a chance to consider this world as does a fish flying, above its element—an elementary milieu totally constituted by supplements, where the element, in other words, is *always lacking*. So, I discovered—and I say this in Platonic terms but from a point of view that opposes me to Plato—that this element was the *hypomnesis*, as that which *gives place* to anamnesis.

Hypomnesis and mortality

Regarding anamnesis, let us recall a scene from *Meno*. Socrates meets Meno, who is on his way to the house of Protagoras to be taught virtue. Socrates proposes to him that he first of all ask what virtue is *for himself*, in order to know if it is truly possible to teach it. To this question of knowing what virtue *is*, Meno responds by proposing *examples* of *various* virtues. Socrates tells him this is not answering the question of knowing what virtue is *as such*: not through *such and such* particular virtue, but virtue as forming the *unity* of all possible virtues, or the *reason* of the *series* of cases that form the examples, the unity of this series, thus the essence of virtue, that is, the *origin* of virtue (that through which it commences). It is then that Meno responds with his famous aporia, whereby Socrates cannot find what he is looking for because either he *does not know it*, and so will not *recognize* it if he finds it, or because he *already* knows it, in which case he is only *pretending* to search for it. Socrates responds that in effect he already knew what he was looking for: he knew it at "another time," then he *forgot* it. From then on, cognition is recognition, a remembering—an *anamnesis*.

Phaedrus, as a dogmatic reprise of *Meno* and a simplification of the meaning of the survival of Socrates in death, on the one hand founds the discourse on the immortality of the soul, in *condemning the body* as a *fall from the origin*, a prison of the soul, site of passion, and *cause of forgetting* by the soul of its knowledge of the origin, and, on the other hand, *opposes* anamnesis to *hypomnesis*.

the latter, as a *technics of memory* (and he is concerned here essentially with the writing of books), with the same defects as the body, and in the same way a prison, is for Plato what renders the soul *forgetful*, replacing *true* memory with *artificial* memory, and accentuates *the forgetting of the origin* into which the soul has fallen in its descent into the body.

Hypomnesis is here, very generally, the figure of artifice, of technics as the dead simulacrum of life-as-immortality. Now, in a much earlier dialogue, Plato had Protagoras undertake a discourse on prostheticity in general and on the defects of the body, and, through it, of mortals and of *mortality* properly speaking—of which Protagoras (in the dialogue that bears his name) proposes a genesis, which is also that of the *fundamentally accidental* character of mortals, fruits of a mistake by the Titans, an accident proceeding precisely from a *forgetting*: Zeus, having asked Prometheus to bring into the day the living beings that are not immortals, hands him all the qualities, the *dunameis*, to distribute to the living. Epimetheus, who is charged with this distribution, *forgets* to save a quality for man, for which Prometheus tries to compensate by *stealing* fire, that is, technics—a theft that is a passage to the act, an attempt, *in vain*, to *make up for* the lack of a quality, in other words the *default of origin*, which from then on afflicts we mortals.

This accidental forgetting, generator of prostheses and artifices making up for a lack of origin, is equally the origin of hypomnesis, to which Plato will later oppose the anamnesis of the origin. In opposition to the metaphysics arising in the *Phaedrus*, the myth of the fault of Epimetheus says that *at the origin there is only an originary default of origin*, and *man, without qualities, only exists by default*: he *becomes*.

The extra-ordinary in the absence of world

A passage to the act plunged me accidentally into a profoundly philosophical situation, which was in its turn a passage from potential to act—a reminiscence through interruption of the action and suspension of the conditions of ordinary life. This was the beginning of an experience of the *extra-ordinary*. I believe the experience of the extra-ordinary is essential to philosophy: it is the meaning of Socrates' shamanism, of his famous *daimon*. It is also the reversal of the natural attitude in Husserl's phenomenology. For five years I had this experience of the extra-ordinary because I was confronted with the *limits* of the conditions of intellective life, being held above the ordinary social surface of those conditions. I almost grabbed hold of the extra-ordinary, as an ordinarily invisible milieu suddenly considered as such—but in the night of my ignorance, groping, it appeared to me to constitute those conditions of experience that cannot be found in experience, because they condition it.[8]

Deprived of an "exterior milieu," my "interior milieu" took on that incommensurable depth and weight sought after by mystics and, more generally, by ascetics. But it is also and just as much *in its absence*, and in the most intimate and secret hollow [*creux*] of the "interior milieu," that the "exterior milieu" is constituted *as irreducible*—and thus I was testing a Husserlian lesson[9] but, as we will see, *a contrario*.[10] Absent, the world *reigned* in my cloister like "the absence of all bouquet."[11] After a few months of incarceration I had written, above the small table where I worked and ate, this verse by Mallarmé:

On no fruits here does my hunger feast,
But finds in their learnèd lack the self-same taste.[12]

As the days passed, I was discovering that there is no interior milieu, but only, remaining here in my cell and *under their mnesic shape*, in a sense in a hollow, the remains, the defaults, the artifices of which the world consists and through which it finds its consistence. I no longer lived in the world, but rather in the absence of a world, which presented itself here not only as a default, but as that which is *always* in default, and as *a necessary default* [un défaut qu'il faut]—rather than as a lack [*manque*].

And, inversely, *for want of these remains producing a default,* there had been nothing else: I *was* woven only out of these *remains.*

Because, finally, the exterior milieu being interrupted and suspended, being in default, in reality there was for me no interior milieu, but rather *its reduction to an exterior milieu itself reduced to an absolute minimum* of that which remained of it in my memory, constituting my interminable recollection via the fabric of my memories—what Husserl called secondary retentions—and which would become for me the material not only of a desperate recollection but also of an anamnesis, of a work of reminiscence, in the properly philosophical sense of the word.

My freedom, hypomneses, and the necessity of the world

From these remains of the world, I gathered material for a reminiscence of the *necessity* of the world—and, in fact, of its properly *irreducible* character. This was certainly a reminiscence or a reactivation from out of those remains, *but,* somewhat like Husserl's analysis of the origin of geometry, this reactivation of the world was not possible other than *via the intermediary of that which would permit me in a way to figure this world ideally,* just as for example Meno's slave figures the geometric ideal in the sand: by relying *on the hypomneses of books read and words written.*

Because the world in which the exterior milieu consisted had not completely disappeared *in its very exteriority* (or I would have gone mad): *I reconstituted it, each day,* through what I would much later name *tertiary retentions,*[13] that is, through hypomnesic traces.

This exteriority was irreducible, which means I could not reach (myself in) it (the interior is nothing without the exterior, the difference between the two being an illusion—obviously necessary, and even insurmountable), but it was within my power to reconstitute it. Such were my freedom, my intimacy, and my secret.

Very quickly, I had the presence of mind to begin to read and write, secreting around me an *intimate* hypomnesic milieu (which was nevertheless already on the way to becoming *public*), at once *secret,* cryptic, and yet already *publishable:* I constituted a *world* that would become, over the years and beyond the period of my incarceration, my philosophy.

If this had not happened, I would have become insane or totally asocial. Because if we are constituted by retentions that remain within us in the absence of the world, these retentions produce *protentions* that are desires for actions, *actual* forms of being-in-the-world. I had found the way to suspend these protentions, because I had transferred them to my unceasing effort to consider the element while being myself maintained outside of it—through fabricating that other element which was in the process of becoming "my philosophy," a pure fabric of hypomneses, of which I daily deposited traces on paper, like a snail sliming along a wall.

The fragility of freedom

Prison is asceticism *without end*—with the exception of micro-interruptions such as visits and, when the time comes, day-release. I ended up being afraid of (while also desiring) these micro-interruptions to the *silence* of which asceticism consists. I even avoided, as much as possible, the "promenades" that broke the silence I had learned to love. When one begins to systematically practice the experience of one's preindividual lived milieu (having become accessible to oneself beyond the context of the world), as an almost palpable milieu (a little like the way in which a hand placed outside the window during high-speed driving causes air to be perceived as a liquid), having thus totally suspended all relation to a meaningful milieu other than that which one carries and reactivates within oneself, or other than that toward which one deliberately heads (such as the book one reads, or rather devours, or the book one writes)—now, if one is all of a sudden confronted with micro-interruptions to this asceticism, then, paradoxically, one suffers terribly: one discovers that, in fact, to be "free" is a suffering. It is suffering because, most of the time, it produces itself not as liberty but precisely as alienation. One perceives with astonishment that, in that cell, one is much more free, or at least that liberty is much more *accessible* there, much purer, appearing then essentially as *fragility*, as what is *intrinsically* fragile, that which must be made the object of the whole of one's care, of a veritable cult, of a culture. This culture, which I have named, after Epictetus, my *melete*.

The silence out of which a voice arises

My *melete* was in reality an ensemble of disciplines. I would, for example, throughout those five years, begin each day by reading Mallarmé—I arose as soon as I awoke, to avoid those uncontrollable protentions that would occur as the waking reveries of the morning. Reading a poem, or reading and rereading a prose text, usually for half an hour, not so as to learn it by heart but to *understand* it.

More generally, my *melete* came from readings leading to prolonged writing exercises in different modes, which came to form veritable reading methods, which consisted in a process by which the texts read were catalogued, then transformed into commentaries, and finally consisted of writing, in which these remains of the world were reassembled: thus was *produced* reminiscence.

In the evening, I read novels.

I lived only in language, and uniquely in written language. I spoke only very rarely. I did not like it; I didn't like it anymore. I had learned to love the silence through which I could listen to what always arose so long as I knew how to wait: an other voice, a soliloquy in which it was not me who was speaking, but the other me, which I called *myself-an-other* [moi-l'autre], the other *of* myself, the other that I *carried* in me, which I became, as if I had been weighed down with what Socrates had ascribed as the task of the maieutician.

Language, in abandoning its communicative function, opened itself fully to its significance, or rather *as* significance, as if it turned itself over to its vocation of signifying, suddenly proliferating. It *made signs*, literally, sometimes to the point of madness. I listened and tried to take note of everything I heard or read. It happened with an absolute necessity. It signified, almost as if it spoke by itself, and, from that point of view, I am obviously tempted to speak of "vocation": it resembled what the tradition considers to be that of which a vocation consists. It was a matter of a voice [*vocare*]. This impersonal voice, which was not the language of communication, was the language of pure significance of which Blanchot spoke regarding Char in *The Beast of Lascaux*. When that language began to "speak," to signify, I had the feeling of entering into a state of ultralucidity. It was a kind of passion, and it was in these exceptional conditions that I encountered the Greek passion for language and the question of *logos* that arises there, a passion and a question that were also a state of exception and an origin: ours, insofar as we philosophize today, in potential or in act. But I came to the position that this originary Greek passion was, as well, a default of origin—as Husserl glimpsed at the end of his life, it was hypomnesically constituted by default, by this default that the hypomnesic technique of writing is.

Much later, I compared my position with Husserl's thoughts on soliloquy in *Logical Investigations*. But I did this on the basis of frequent preparatory readings of Plato and his discourse on *dianoia*, dialectic as the dialogue of the soul with itself, in a context where, for me—rigorously experimenting with *dianoia*, understanding it in order to criticize dialectic as Plato wanted to establish it—it was *first of all a matter of fighting* against the *bad soliloquy*: the hell lived by those who, as one says, talk to themselves, those whom one sees everywhere these days in the streets, those who have lost their spirit, overcome by the harshness of life.

This was, then, how I undertook to practice philosophy, as the experience of a silence in which a voice arose, as a soliloquy sustained by the hypomneses of writing, anamnesically reconstituting language as that which does not allow itself to be understood except through the trial of a cloistered asceticism and an absolute solitude, language that is rarely produced in the dialectic of a dialogue between two, in the social dialectic, which has almost always become, today, unfortunately for us, pure chatter, if not a system of cretinization.

In that soliloquy of extremities, on the verge of talking to myself but just before that point, on the edge of that quasi-madness of extreme thoughts, of final ends and profound roots, hypomnesis was my *safeguard.*

To give place: The invention of locality

I thus discovered what one calls in philosophy the *phenomenological epokhe*—the suspension of the world, of the thesis of the world, that is, of the spontaneous belief in the existence of the world, which constitutes in Husserl's language the natural attitude—what I previously called ordinary life. I discovered this philosophical theory and practice by chance and by accident, long before studying it in the works of Husserl: I *deduced* it from the situation, I practiced it, in a way, empirically and savagely. When I discovered it formulated and theorized by phenomenology, I found myself in a state of unimaginable excitement. I believe that Granel, who accompanied me throughout this adventure, was also enthused, and that he had the impression of witnessing a perfectly singular experience, but at the same time he also found himself at times disarmed: my situation often made me resistant to traditional readings of what he rightly liked to call "the tradition."

Then, by chance, thanks to Gérard Granel himself, thanks to the books, the paper, to the knowledge of writing and reading taught to me by the Republic, for which I here give thanks as a child cherishing its mother, through this chance issuing from struggles that were conducted for literacy, notably by philosophers, struggles that would prove one can conduct a *politics of the passage to the philosophical act, if you will,* by the chance of everything that I will shortly call the *already-there,* which left me the legacy of that fortunate heritage, I was able to pass from the empirical practice of the *epokhe,* of the suspension, to a practice that was reasoned, methodical, and to an "apodictic" vocation or pretension.

I was able to enter philosophy properly speaking by accident, therefore, but also *thanks to the laws of the City:* the spirit of the laws of the French Republic meant there was a library in this old prison.

These laws and that which is today, through the state, still preserved as their spirit will, *I hope*, in the years to come, not find their destruction, but on the contrary their *anamnesis, in a sense their renewal.*
I thus passed into philosophical thought, that is, apodictic thought. *Apodictic* means without *deixis*, on the other side of *deixis*, outside *deixis*, outside context: outside milieu, without *here-and-now*. *Deixis* is, in Greek, the here-and-now, it is *that which shows itself* as here-and-now, the *monstrative* site of what Aristotle called the *tode ti*, the that-which-is-here. The apodictic is the *demonstrative*, which does not give itself other than through being torn from context, from local determinations, and, as such, the apodictic *already* supposes a suspension—if not that of the world, at least that of its here-and-now, its *locality*.

So, in the suspension of the world, and in its apodictic residue, I found first an absence of world, this "learnèd lack," which, as such (*a lack*), is rather a *fault* [défaut] and a *necessity* [il faut], that which *gives* and *gives place*, rather than what "lacks place." The lack, in this case, is the inability to know how to live this absence, in this absence; it does not know how to find the learning necessitated by default, *that is, to invent it.* In the impossibility, in the unsupportability of the absence of world, quite close to the *un-world* [immonde], I found the world as *irreducible* locality, and as locality itself constituted, in all circumstances, but invisibly, just as water is absent to a fish, *by default, by the default,* and even *as* default, for example, that default of pronunciation which we hear in a foreign accent.

I posed the default as *that which every locality expresses, in its guise and according to its place:* as originary default of origin, inasmuch as *a locality is always artifactually and prosthetically constituted*—and, in my situation then and there, reconstituted *by* and *in* that which *remained* of a "milieu" despite everything, granting *me* in the end *a* place still, an *ensemble of remains* that I wanted to save and that I therefore reconstituted hypomnesically, fighting against the finitude of my memory, against that which I later called, with Derrida, commenting on Husserl, my *retentional fini-*

tude. With these remains, hypomnesically transformed, I produced a new world, I gave place to another place, where I finally found what I would call the *virtue* of prison.

I discovered, through the apodictic path, a *necessity* of the world (that which is *necessary* of the default), an *irreducibility of deicticity* or, to put it another way, that which nevertheless could never, without doubt, be *apodictically demonstrated*—except *by default.*

I believe that to speak of the necessity of the *tie* that the default is, its *"it must"* ["il faut"], is the heart of the question of Socrates' *Apology* (the default is first of all mortality) and of *Crito* (where the law is necessary for me to be condemned), even the *Phaedo*—because that also has to do with "dying and wanting to be dead," as Phaedo says to Socrates in prison, which nevertheless does not at all mean that Socrates speaks of the immortality of the soul: the *Phaedo* concerns on the contrary the *acceptance* of mortality, which is piety, which means also and even initially *accepting the laws* of the City. This is *philia* as love, to the death, of the City: right up to the hemlock.

This by-default is what I experimented with through my *melete* and my *dianoia* with the Platonic hypomneses that form the *Dialogues,* against Plato's phantasm of pure liberty, opposed to all alienation and all default, to all default posed as alienation—and I did it while not ceasing to read Plato, in Plato's *absence,* dare I say it: there, in his absences, such as in the *Symposium,* is revealed his immense impact *after* the Platonic evasion that betrays Socrates, and which unfortunately consists in *opposing* the soul to the body, and anamnesis to hypomnesis, to dogmatize the immortality of the soul, that is, to refuse to accept its being-*by-default* or, to put it another way, its *being-in-becoming.* This is, in effect, what gets metaphysics underway, and against which I struggled and fought throughout those five years.

The idiom of that which signifies

The laws of the City always have this character of locality that marks them as laws of *this* city, index of contingency and accidentality, from which fact proceeds the Athenian decision to condemn Socrates to death by hemlock. This contingency is that which marks itself and remarks itself, in the first place in the irreducibility of the idiomatic character of language, in that its significance comes solely from signifying and making signs, through which language does not cease to *reinvent* itself. Whether speaking, even alone or silently, or writing, I am already within that jurisdiction: I always belong to a here and now, to a locality, no matter what. Even when imprisoned, I belong to *local-ity* by default, and in default *as* locality, because it is *still* my language that constitutes me, insofar as it is idiomatic. And all those *retentions,* which are themselves traces of that which is in default because it is *no longer there*—it is no longer there as that which must be there, precisely as *that which makes sense,* idiom, locality, that is, *being-there*—present suddenly and completely differently that *which is no longer there*: the world, not as an unformed, vague, amorphous exterior, nor simply the sum of physical laws constituting things and beings. The world, *precisely* insofar as it *signi-fies* and can only do so *from* its local-ity.

From then on I tried to isolate the degrees of localities by diverse *imaginary variations* and *signifying practices.*

There was the most local level of the idiomacity of my soliloquy, which I cultivated and maintained through the artificial retentional milieu of my hypomneses, constituting in its isolated facticity a here and now where, finally, *something always happened* and, even, *more than ever.* This was because I remained temporal in remaining idiomatic, and thus I never finished becoming. The factical world was my whole world, but in which took place an intense signifying production, a profusion of new enunciations, inherited from the already-there of my knowledge held in memory, by my "secondary retentions," and maintained through the tertiary retentions of my reading and of my writing, which substituted for absent things insofar as they themselves *give support.*

And there was the level of what I call *the most-ample-locality: mortal-ity as* ethos *of all mortals,* that is, of the desiring and signifying beings that we are; the locality that for example ties me, between beasts and immortals, to Lascaux—the giving-place that I *share* with Lascaux.

Between these extremities lie innumerable variations forming so many modes of constitution of the *we* where we are as *I, idiolects and dialects*, but also still unthought networks of new modes of "deterritorializing."

This is what led me to the question of the default in general but, more particularly, of the default that the question of prosthesis poses, the question of the artifact, and of substitution, and so on. All locality would in fact be constituted from such prostheses, where idiomaticity would be the symbolic but also artifactual elementarity of that supplementarity.

And in fact I was only able to *hold*—and continue to *have a place*—through constituting and reconstituting daily the artificial locality of my writing and my reading.

Significance and insignificance

The conditions of the constitution of the world appear in the absence of the world in particular as the impossibility of *choosing*—one's clothes, one's home, one's friends, the use of one's time, and so on—and consequently of articulating and arranging. The world is *being-toward-the-world*—I then began to enter into *Being and Time*, and to begin building, dare I say it, a *soli-loquy* [soliloque] with Heidegger—and this world is the fabric or the framework of *signifying practices*, as well as being that which is framed and woven *by* these practices.

Because finally, in effect, that which ties all those questions that invaded me in the immobility and silence of soliloquy, beginning from the first day of my imprisonment, is in all its diverse facets the *question of significance* and of its *combat with insignificance*, with itself, in other words, and the experience of this intimate and secret difference, which appears or does not appear, or which disappears, in things and between things, and which *changes everything* about things.

Everyone has had this experience, and in truth has it ceaselessly, whether consciously or not: one desires or waits for or considers an object, a good, a being; then the object, the good, or the being, being there, effaces itself, becomes indifferent, even oppressive, disgusting, eclipsed—nothing.

In prison I *permanently* and in a kind of *pure way* had the experience of the remains that framed me and that in the end I *am*. But if others can *cover over* this experience, this is so only to the degree that it produces itself—which is what permits one to flee it, as happens in the ordinary world. It was posed there before me and as *the very experience* of the *me*: I could not *avoid* noting that, in fact, it is *in me* and *by me* that everything *passes* and is *passed*; it is not the thing that is insignificant because, yesterday, it was significant; and since I am alone with it and *nothing around us has changed*, I cannot ignore it: it is I, as *living memory*, who have *transformed* myself since yesterday, while around me everything is still as it was yesterday and as it will be tomorrow.

In prison, that which, today, is very prominent and consistent, laden with meaning and, in that sense, "significant," never fails to become, tomorrow, indifferent, totally insignificant, and the very opposite of what it was—*at least insofar as I have not understood that precisely from these facts comes this other fact that there is nothing insignificant in itself*, and that *what can be insignificant are not the things themselves, or in themselves, but the relation I have or rather that I do not have with those things*, such as I *articulate* and *arrange* them.

In undertaking this ordeal I came to understand that there is no abstract significance—that is, outside of a signifying *material* and a signifying *practice*—and that I alone am responsible for whether there is signification or not. From then on I adopted a principled attitude, according to which *my task consisted of finding significance in the insignificant*. I posed in principle that there is *nothing* insignificant other than myself when, precisely, I do not want to become myself-another, when I do not want to allow myself to be altered, *to allow myself to individuate*, through the signifying of the other (other thing, other me).

And I understood that significance demands frequentation, the frequenting of a practice. One does not arrive at the significance of a language, for example, in which one does not have a *sustained relation where one individuates oneself,* in a language that one does not speak, no more than one arrives at the significance of a music that one does not frequent assiduously—like the poetry of Mallarmé, which gives itself only to the *patient.*[14]

It is *thus* that I came to impose upon myself and to systematically practice my disciplines, my *melete*—where I discovered that *significance has a part essentially tied to memory:* objects and, more generally, the "significants"—the utterances, books, signs and symbols, objets d'art, and all that which frames the unity of human milieus—only appear to me as *echoes* of my memory. It is insofar as they respond to an *expectation* of my memory, a protention, that they can signi-fy, make *signs,* make signs *to me.* From then on it was a question of learning to *cultivate high expectations.*

I understood also that the opposing couple of *signifier* and *signified* was not the right question, and that this was what Saussure had got bogged down in—and with him the whole of structuralism. I encountered, but by a wholly other path, the enterprise of Jacques Derrida, whose *Of Grammatology* I read avidly.

The alter *in the* ego

Thus was constituted the question of my reminiscence.

But this quite clearly had another source, that of the memorious reconsideration of that which brought me there, leaving me with a unique question: how could I at that point *no longer have loved* the world, have found it *so insignificant,* that I had taken the risk, in passing to the act, of finding myself completely removed, immobilized and imprisoned in that cell, with no way out except that of finding in myself the resources that would give me access to such questions, and finding there a sense of things and the desire for this world?

It is out of this first question that the question of reminiscence emerged, instructed by the material of my past life, and as the question of signifying practices that it was a matter of reinventing from out of the insignificance into which I had fallen, to the point of passing to the act, finding myself, presently alone, *solely responsible* for my past and my future.

I then understood that signifying practices constitute frameworks, repetitions, which I called texts in the sense of fabrics [*tissus*], in a sense that is thus not only linguistic but grammatical, that is, *retentional,* and that they are the *supports* of making-world. The fabric of signifying practices that forms the material of the world, which organizes and programs all social behavior, can obviously weaken, rip, decay: I can perfectly well enter into an attitude of inattention to the world, and thus of insignificance, even of dereliction. And it is to the extent that the world appears insignificant to me, and in a way does not appear to me at all, that I am *myself* insignificant—and I know this, and I suffer from it: difficult freedom. I very often saw this possibility of decay in prison, almost every time I left my cell (and first of all in myself), and I constantly felt it as the danger facing me, myself, at the limit. But I anticipated it above all as the danger to come from refound liberty or, rather, from disincarceration.

Isolated, I was able to experiment, observe, and note how I was able to adopt an attitude of availability, a disposition, or, on the contrary, to occupy a position and make myself unavailable to that to which I opposed myself, and how I was able to make myself available or unavailable depending on those practices that I did or did not take up in the diverse signifying fields that were mine.

With nothing there for me, *everything I lacked sent me back to those practices,* which, all of a sudden, *no longer had any material support.* This is how I understood that signifying practices are forms of discipline, more or less perceptible, and that if I did not want to tumble into madness—that is, into a-significance, which is much worse that insignificance—*it was necessary that I impose on myself a melete,* not only as an ensemble of rules and maxims but, especially, of *practices in signifying fields.*

So, the access to the "transcendental" subject, the goal of all *epokhe,* appeared therefore impossible *without the other,* that other being itself inaccessible without signifying practices: outside of the outside. *Thus there was no inside.* Because what shined brilliantly in the absence of the world was *the alterity of the other*, and in the *signifying soli-logue* I tried to maintain with myself, it was *the alterity that, still there by default, appeared vital*, and which I had to find *in myself* in altering myself through those practices by which I grasped, little by little, that others in the world are there to give me access, through them, to *my* alterity, to my future. To my individuation.

It was no longer a matter of reaching an *alter ego*, but *the alter without the ego*, the alterity of an other that was not constituted *from me*, but *of which I am first constituted*, as "myself-an-other" [*"moi-autre"*] rather than "my-self" [*"moi-même"*], and to which the outside *gives place*. This outside was just as much the question of the *already-there*, concretized through tertiary retention: traces, hypomnesic productions.

I am essentially my outside, which is something *spatial*, and that inevitably means also *hypomnesically* already-there; but it is therefore also—and immediately—*temporal*, since it is constituted in the *already*, and *memorially*. In this *remainder* that in prison cannot cease, even when there is apparently no longer anything else—that is, when time no longer seems to flow—space appeared to me, however, to constitute time or, rather, to reconstitute it, in a kind of originary *après-coup*. And that meant I had to learn to think *before* the opposition of space and time.

Much later I discovered that this question of the already-there, which I have learned to formulate through Heidegger, and which I formalized for the first time in 1980 through the concept of idiotext, was also the question of what Simondon called the preindividual. My individuation, as becoming-other, can only be the recollection of my retentional already-there, hypomnesically supported, and which, insofar as it is charged with protentions, is also an individuation of the *we* in which is constituted *the alter without the ego*.

Significance and locality form, ultimately, a single question. I cannot find the *virtue of necessity* other than in the accidents and the contingencies that befall me: *virtue is outside of me. It is my*

*outside, the outside. I can only find necessity in a milieu, and only this
gives me access to myself, which means there is no difference inside/out-
side.* Having met with this realization, it governed my subsequent
reading and comprehension of *Of Grammatology*, a text that was
crucial for me in relation to this question.

When I say that the necessity of milieu—that I have to *invent*
it and that I experiment by default with it—cannot be found except *by myself*, I say the *same thing as when I speak of significance
and insignificance*, which is my pure responsibility. It is only my
relation to the thing that gives it significance or not: this is what
was shown so well by Barthes, who uncovered in any element
whatever of daily life its signifying force in the world, contrary
to the insignificance that it ordinarily seemed to constitute. The
extra-ordinariness of the world is what is found by one who knows
how to go beyond the insignificance of things, things that one had
rendered ordinary by tying them up in a nonrelation, forgetting
them. We have here returned to the question of anamnesis.

The material of spirit—before prison

Before I arrived in prison, I had no philosophy, in the sense
that I knew practically nothing about it, but nevertheless I had a
position, an attitude or a philosophical disposition, which passed
precisely through *materialism*, which was *constituted politically*—I
had been a member of the Communist Party—and which was not
therefore philosophical in its origin: *I had the conviction that ma-
teriality is primary and conditions everything*; I therefore considered
myself an *anti-idealist* and, as such, I believed that *philosophers were
necessarily on the wrong side*, to the degree that they are inevitably
on the side *of the interpretation of the world and not of changing the
state of things.*

True philosophy, that is, *philosophy in action(s)*, that was politics;
and true politics, that was materialist philosophy. My opponents
were those who belonged to idealism, identified through Marx's
aphorism condemning the interpretation of the world and appeal-
ing for its transformation through *acts*.

I cannot say that today I am a materialist in that sense, but I must say that I remain a materialist, in the sense of a materialism that does not deny the spirit, but which poses that the spirit, while not reducible to matter, is always conditioned by it. "Not reducible to matter" signifies that there is a process, produced in matter but irreducible to physical laws, or even biological ones: there is a play of mnemonic layers that are at the same time biological, psychic, and hypomnesic, and which require formalizations for which the resources of the natural sciences remain irreducibly insufficient.

I preserve the word *spirit* to qualify this process insofar as it concerns a process of *return* where, in particular, what returns is moved by what I call the unreal *consistence* of that which, while certainly *not existing*—for example, justice—is irreducible, and does not cease, therefore, to *consist*: one cannot renounce it, and it is an essential motor of all human life—and the condition of desire. That which *con-sists* therefore does not cease to return as *in-sistence*, legacy of prior generations and responsibility of a heritage.

Twenty-five years later

I followed this path for five years, in the patient immobility of silence, in what I call the *virtue of prison*, to prepare myself, between 1978 and 1983, for a *return to the world, more worthy, more necessary, more intelligent. The more time passed, the more I feared falling back into that world*, the more I sensed that the world refound would not be immediately welcoming.

And unfortunately, in the twenty-five years that have passed since that epoch, the world has in effect revealed itself to be appallingly inhospitable, as if I found myself in front of you having returned to square one.

It appeared to me, in effect, as without doubt it does to many among you, that everything seems to be organized to encourage the attitude in which insignificance dominates, or even a-significance. This is what I call the organization of the *loss of individuation*. Now, this is full of terrifying passages to the act, in relation to which one asks if a maieutic is still possible today.

Twenty-five years after the passage to the act that led me toward philosophy through acting—years that reconnected me to those who, alarmed and overwhelmed by life, stupefied by marketing and the media, appeared to me so estranged not only from philosophy through acting but from all potential vocation to philosophize, that one ends up asking if the unity of a *we* is still possible—I ask myself what is the unity of my own life, if it has one.

In October 2002 Marie Alphant suddenly directed me back to that question of the *forgetting of why* one does what one *does*, in suddenly making it necessary for me to say from *where comes* and *from what proceeds*, in its accidental sources, the material of what I now call "my thought." So, it became problematic for me to live in the occultation of my past, even if that occultation was part of my existence by choice: I wanted to play the role not of ex-convict but first of all of philosopher, discretely, out of this material, in remaining *faithful* to it but, in a sense, without citing my sources or resources.

Faithful, unfaithful

Now, the question of fidelity is an aporia. One cannot be faithful to the unity and the identity of what remains constant throughout the alterities of the diverse characters one will have been and played, sometimes without knowing it, without noticing it, and which results from the accidental character of existence.

It is therefore perhaps not by chance that around 1995 I set to work on the *Critique of Pure Reason*, to plough through the Paralogisms of the *ego* and the question of the unity of consciousness.

I have had successive lives, if not multiple personalities. I have changed my life several times. But what is it to change one's life? And is it possible? In truth, this is the question of the fidelity of commitments [*engagements*]. Being-in-becoming, which is our default, immediately opens the question of fidelity, that is, of faith. One must change and, as the saying goes, "Only imbeciles don't change. . . . " And at the same time one must *remain*. Be and *remain* faithful. Be faithful to what remains; remain faithful to the remains. Now this is what makes retentional finitude difficult: the fact that memory fails. Being fragile and fallible, memory is unfaithful. This question, to which I have often bound myself—the relation between this question of fidelity to oneself and the infidelity of oneself, of the self and its means, precisely, the problem of the means through which is permitted the dulling of retentional finitude—has not yet released me, since it is henceforth a matter for me of also remaining faithful to an experience of what was most near, and *as that which is so near to the vile* [l'immonde].

The question of time is perhaps, like the question of the unity of consciousness, what has really posed itself to me ever since 1978. It has posed itself in numerous ways: partly as a recollection leading me toward reminiscence; partly as the experience of time as flowing in an eminently variable way according to the conditions into which one is existentially thrown, above all in the *unchanging* context of incarceration; and, then, as the hypomnesic dimension of anamnesis, as the originarily technical dimension of time; and, finally, as the question of the unity and nonunity of being, which was the subject of the book I published in 2001.[15]

From the moment one is in a process of reminiscence, one is in the reconstitution of hypomnesis, and thus in the *après-coup*. Now, the *après-coup* is the irreducible creator of phantasms and fictions. It is impossible for me not to make fiction in the course of speaking. How then to accept this situation of making fiction without accepting lies, that is, infidelity to oneself? That is, equally, how to accept this without accepting it as infidelity to others, to those whom one addresses? Everything I have said to you this evening is subject to this context of the *après-coup*. I believe that it is absolutely impossible to resolve or reduce these difficulties. I believe the only worthwhile fidelity is one that tackles this problem of the *après-coup* head on. In a certain way, the religious do it. The problem is that monotheism does it in the mode of guilt. And this is precisely what must be avoided. Nothing, in effect, above all at this moment, is more conducive of passages to undesirable acts than culpabilization.

To the law

My life will have been a succession of lives, as if I have had several lives, a multiplicity of stories and roles. I have not ceased to have changes of life.

I have never philosophized, if I have ever philosophized, other than through the ordeal of this succession of roles I have been able to occupy—and of the vertiginous variety of viewpoints that *remain* within me.

I carry this succession as the very mark of the default of origin—which is necessary—of which these successive and accidental roles are masks, *persona* that have been *needed*, that I became as necessary, and that were only justified, if they ever were, in the *après-coup* of my fragile liberty, in my fallible fidelity to the default of origin—*to the law*.

To Love, to Love Me, to Love Us:
From September 11 to April 21

I dedicate this lecture[1] to the electors of the National Front, to whom I feel close. I feel close to them because they are people who suffer and who cause me to suffer. They cause me to suffer because in the proximity of their suffering, I feel them infinitely distanced from me—and I feel infinitely far from them. I feel that this distance is our lost community. This distance is paradoxically the vanishing point of our common suffering and, as such, our proximity. What is common to us is the feeling of absolute separation. But this concerns not only our common suffering, but also the suffering that separates us. If I feel close to those people who suffer while they also make me suffer, if I suffer with them, I do not suffer only because they make me suffer. I suffer also with them from that which makes them suffer.

§ 1   The destruction of primordial narcissism

Narcissism and insecurity

The violence and insecurity in which we live—as much as they are exploited to the point of fantasy, or even deliberately manipulated—engage above all a question of narcissism, and result from a process of loss of individuation. It is a matter of narcissism in the sense of someone like Richard Durn, assassin of a *we*—to assassinate members of a municipal council, the official representatives of a *we*, is to assassinate a *we*—who suffered terribly from not existing, from not having, he said, a "feeling of existing."[2] When he looked in the mirror he saw only an immense nothing. This was revealed by the publication of his personal diary in *Le Monde*. Durn affirmed that he had a need to "do evil at least once in his life, to have the feeling of existing."[3]

Richard Durn suffered from a *structural privation of his primordial narcissistic capacities*.[4] I call "primordial narcissism" that structure of the psyche which is indispensable for functioning, that part of self-love which can sometimes become pathological, but without which any capacity for love would be impossible. Freud speaks of primary narcissism, but that is not what I am referring to. Primary narcissism designates infantile self-love, a precocious phase of sexuality. Freud also speaks of secondary narcissism, which survives into adulthood, but this is still not primordial narcissism, which is without doubt closer to what Lacan calls the "mirror phase." Now, there is a primordial narcissism *of the we just as there is of the I*: for the narcissism of my *I* to function, there must be a narcissism of the *we* onto which it can project itself. Richard Durn, failing to develop his narcissism, saw in the municipal council the reality of an alterity that made him suffer, that did not return to him any image, and he massacred it.

The narcissistic structure of a story

> The most important theoretical advance has certainly been the application of the libido theory to the repressing ego. The ego itself came to be regarded as a reservoir of what was described as narcissistic libido from which the libidinal investment in objects flowed out, and into which they could be once more withdrawn.[5]

This is Freudian energy: the ego is an energetic process having a potential. This potential circulates, and it so happens that when it functions badly, narcissism engenders narcissistic troubles. Freud in fact has a list: early dementia, paranoia, and melancholy. Narcissistic conditions that are diverse forms of neuroses also exist.

It is, however, in a very specific sense that we live in an epoch of great narcissistic suffering, characterized notably by the suffering of the narcissism of the *we*, by a kind of *sickness of the we*. I am not an *I* other than to the extent that I am part of a *we*. An *I* and a *we* are processes of individuation. As such, as processes of individuation, the *I* and the *we* have a history. This is not merely to say that each *we* is a different history; it contains the additional sense that the conditions of the individuation of the *we*, throughout the course of human history, transform themselves.

The conditions of individuation at the start of the twenty-first century are different from those of the fifth century B.C. (the birth of the Greek city), which are themselves different from those of Cro-Magnon man, which are in turn different from those at the birth of the primitive horde of which Freud speaks in *Totem and Taboo*. These processes of individuation and their evolutions have their own conditions, the conditions for the passage from one phase of the process of individuation to another, of a *we*, and through it, of the *I*. These conditions for the evolution of individuation are mnemotechnics or mnemotechnologies. Today we are enduring an enormous suffering of this individuation and this narcissism, a collapse of the necessary primordial narcissism of the *I* and the *we*, and the *I* in the *we*. This suffering occurs insofar as mnemotechnics and mnemo-techno-logies (which govern all the processes of human individuation) have passed into the sphere of industrial exploitation.

Narcissism, consumption, and passage to the act

Industrial exploitation poses problems regarding the limits of what is possible with industry's resources. We are, today, insofar as we are *I*s, essentially targeted as consumers. Now, a consumer does not have the right to say *I*: a consumer is no longer either an *I* or *we*, because he or she is reduced to a *they*:[6] the consumer is depersonalized, disembodied, in principle and in structure. Consumption—as an epoch of the system related to what I call the process of adoption[7]—tends to confound the *I* and the *we*, to annul the differences between them and thus to transform them into a *they*. The organization of consumption—which consists in *synchronizing* the *I*s to the point of annihilating their differences (because after all an *I* is a diachrony, since I can say *I* only insofar as *my* time is not *your* time)—is what tends to annul the love of self, self-love. In effect, if my singularity is annulled by the synchronization *of my* behavior (that is, *of my consumption*) with the behavior of others (that is, with the consumption of others), this permits the realization of industrial economies of scale.[8] *I* am thereby progressively annulled and, because of this progressive annulment of my *I*, I no longer love myself. Now, if I no longer love myself, I no longer love others, since others are nothing more than the mirror of my self-love: in this consists primordial narcissism. From the moment that I no longer love myself and no longer love others, all transgression becomes possible: there is no longer any limit to my action, which means my action may become a passage to the act of pure madness.

In dedicating this lecture to the electors of the National Front insofar as they suffer—like you and I but perhaps more than you and I—I am saying to you that the unlimited organization of consumption is the organization of the liquidation of narcissism (of which these electors are victims), a liquidation that is the *organization of pure madness,* leading inevitably to suicidal behavior, both individual and collective.

Becoming and future

The liquidation of narcissism, *that is to say, of individuation,* intensifies *terribly* the phenomenon of dis-adjustment that regularly occurs to shake up human societies. Society is always haunted, articulated and worked through by a process of technical transformation, which is at first very slow (lithic industry of the chopper, then, at the rhythm of millions of years, the bi-face tool) but accelerates with sedentarization, then with large empires, and finally with the process of permanent innovation characterizing the industrial society in which we live.

When a technical system transforms, it dis-adjusts social relations and provokes their dis-equilibrium, but this is generally temporary.[9] These dis-equilibriums translate into crises punctuating history, which may be more or less violent. But when these processes of dis-equilibrium linked to technical evolution combine with a *loss of individuation* engendered by the liquidation of the narcissistic potential of the *I* (which has only happened in our own epoch), dis-adjustment attains a limit.

We are talking here prospectively: this prospective is a question of collective intelligence of the future—and therefore of the understanding of the question of time. This is a matter of human time, not the time of the stars. Human time relates to stellar time, yet they are different. Stellar time is entropic, the time of the physical becoming of the expansion of the universe. Human time is negentropic in an extreme sense.[10] It is not only the biological structure of humankind that, as is the case for all living beings, is negentropic. Cultural structures are too, in principle. Human language is therefore constitutionally idiomatic (we will come back to this point). Confounding stellar time with human time reduces negentropic time to entropic becoming, which is contradictory—except in posing the possibility of the "end of times," that is to say, the end of the future (which is far more complex than becoming and also, therefore, more fragile). The possibility of the future is fragile: this is why the end of the future is far more probable than the end of becoming. It is because the future cannot be reduced to becoming (but must on the other hand negotiate with it) that we must fight against all scientism. The reduction of the future to becoming would be its liquidation—it would be the "end of times"—and this is indeed possible. Those who do not want to hear talk of such a possibility do not know how to *discern* that which, *in becoming*, constitutes the *possibility* of the future without confounding it with this becoming.

The articulation of the *I* and the *we*

Human time articulates the *I* with the *we*. I am human only insofar as I am part of a social group. The time of the *I* is not, however, the time of the *we*: it has its place in the time of the *we*, which is conditioned by the time of the *I*s that compose it. The difficulty consists in this tension—and this complexity makes difficult what one calls *collective intelligence* (which reason a priori poses as possibility and necessity).

The question of the articulation of the *I* and the *we* is overdetermined by that of technics. This has always been the case, but in the past it was not perceived. It became perceivable in the nineteenth century and above all in the twentieth, when industrial objects appeared systematically in the form of new objects dedicated to replacing preceding ones. This is what we call consumption [*consommation*]. Now, each day, hundreds of patents are lodged around the world, from which result innumerable new objects, which must be adopted and which make us adopt them.

Marketing, the media, systems of behavioral synchronization, which serve to more or less artificially "sustain" consumption, are technologies of adoption: they make us adopt a new toothpaste, a new washing powder, a new type of mobile phone, a new optional standard in cars. We must consume in order for the economic machine of the global *we* to function. Psychological techniques are developed to make us adopt new products because, a priori, we don't want them. Societies have no spontaneous need for new products. As a general rule, they want to remain as they are, yet they must also transform themselves to survive.

Today, the specific and specifically miserable trait of our epoch is that the articulation of the *I* and the *we* is *hegemonically* submitted to the imperative to adopt the new, according to the mode of consumption.

The process of adoption and what we want

The adoption of new products has grafted itself onto the general process of adoption, at the heart of which the social is constituted. Techniques of adoption, such as marketing, can develop only because of the generally hidden and forgotten fact that society is already a process of adoption. The occlusion of the knowledge that there is always adoption can even take the form of burying thousands and even millions of individuals in mass graves. Ernest Renan, Paul Valéry, and André Leroi-Gourhan, in particular, highlighted the process of adoption. Ernest Renan explains in "What Is a Nation?" that all societies are constituted by immigrants who arrive but do not form part of a *we*, so that one must say that the *we* does not literally exist.[11] Leroi-Gourhan showed this regarding China: China is made up of thousands of different ethnicities that have shaped the past of a *we* that never existed, yet which, in permitting the projection of this phantasmic past, also made possible the projection of a common future. Tocqueville, speaking of America, established that all society is created in this way. But this fictive creation must be hidden because, to be able to adhere to the past, I must *believe* that I belong to this phantasmic past *we*, and therefore make this past mine.

Last year I gave, during the colloquium "Modernity: The New Map of the Times,"[12] the example of my personal case: I am a French citizen, my children are French citizens, but we are called Stiegler, like my paternal grandfather—and my maternal grandfather was called Trautmann. In other words, I recognize in the *sans-culottes* the representatives of my past, and this *remembering* elevates the narcissism of the *we*, even if the past of my grandparents is *not* that of the *sans-culottes*. I adopt my past by integrating the lessons of places of adoption—school and certain other structures—conceived to enable me to adopt it. A common past with you who are French permits me to construct with you a *we* projecting a future, permitting us to say together, "*Our* future: *we* want this, *we* want that."

Until a recent epoch, this process of adopting a past—which is artificial but at the same time permits me to adopt a future—was concealed. Nevertheless, the question of adoption is posed more and more explicitly from the time of the industrial revolution onward, as new objects appear without interruption and with increasing speed, and as the framework of daily life incessantly transforms itself.

For social structures to absorb this incessant novelty, adoptive techniques must be put in place. The problem of adoption is posed as such from then on, and social organization explicitly becomes the organization of adoption or, in other words, the organization of consumption.

Calendarity, cardinality, and fiction

Adoption is that which is presupposed by the constitution of a *we* in general. A *we* is always constituted by calendarity and cardinality. For us to be able to say *we*, we must share the same calendar system and the same cardinal system. If we cannot refer to the same calendar, that is, if we do not share common time, and if we do not have a common representation of the spatial world in which we share systems of orientation—for example, if we cannot read street names, maps, or road signs—we amount to strangers. We have no sense of familiarity with a *we* other than on condition of such a sharing. Today, however, calendarity and cardinality are submitted to the control of global cultural industries.

Calendarity organizes the coming together of the *we*. Sunday was originally a sacred day for Christianity, a day of rest in common. The mass media has turned it into a day for a televisual rendezvous. What is true of days is true of hours. Everyone today recognizes what we call "*20 Heures*," news-time on television. The television channel TF1 has recently seen its share price fall because it purchased at very high cost the broadcast rights for a Zinedine Zidane football match. This star of the French team was supposed to guarantee the channel and its advertisers a record audience, but he injured his knee and his participation in this global sporting encounter became uncertain. *TF1, like all TV stations, derives its value from its capacity to control calendarity*—and the football World Cup is a major rendezvous on the global calendar. To control access to the consciousness of consumers at such events constitutes a fundamental advantage: it ensures in principle very high audience ratings. Yet one can sense the fragility of such a system (if not its absurdity) in the fact that the weakness of a footballer's knee may threaten it.

Submitted to the control of cultural industries, calendrical and cardinal systems are in the process of disintegrating—and this provokes a *loss of individuation* as a consequence of the resulting *destruction of primordial narcissism*. A calendrical system and a cardinal system direct us to something beyond the calculable—and, moreover, in sport, one still exploits a kind of adoration of the inestimable, of the *exception*, of the unique event. The calendar even directs us back to the divine, or even to the exceptional foundational event of politics, or even to both at the same time, and in any case to an exceptional event that stands above the present as an excess. The power of belonging to a group requires the projection of an always fictive unity of this group, and this is always a fiction that narrates an exception. The power of saying *we* requires that I "fiction" a past that is not mine, and this allows me to fiction a future that I hope will belong to us—me, those close to me [*mes proches*], my children, and, from one to the next [*de proche en proche*], *you*.

Desire and infinity

This future that I fiction—that is, which I desire and fantasize—I will without doubt never see: it will very probably never happen. But I need that which will never take place in the mode of a fiction, in which I propose that, despite everything, it *will be*, in the form of an *absolute* future: a future that will always remain still to come, a sort of *pure future*. This fiction is called, for example, the messiah. It is only possible infinitely: it involves desire, individual desire, which is indissociably from the *we* and of the *we*, indissociable from the desire for a *we*, desire for the possibility of saying *we*. Desire is structurally related to infinity. Freud tells us, correctly, that libidinal energy is limited. But for that limited libidinal energy to function, *it is necessary that I fantasize my energy as unlimited*. This is merely a fiction, but *without this fiction there would be no desire*. What I love I love without limit, without condition: I cannot love it other than in a manner that is (phantasmatically) unlimited. That which I love and those whom I love, you, that is, us insofar as we are capable of forming a *we*—all this I love, and I love it (and I love you) *infinitely*. I love to the infinite. I love only to the infinite, as one says, "to the infinitive." Without which no *we* is possible.

This is nothing but a fiction. There is no infinite love—no *we* as the origin of an *I*—that is not a phantasm. But I repeat: without this fiction (that is, without the *default of origin* that is the fiction of desire), the *we* is impossible. We become less than "barbarians," beasts and, worse than beasts, a pure destructive power. We become, literally, diabolical. This is what the question of *philia* in the *Nicomachean Ethics* teaches and means.[13] And if I had the time, I would show you how and why, as a result of what I have just said, the *we*, like the *I*, must be capable of a primordial narcissism: how it needs symbols, that is, auto-erotic fetishes, in which it can be reflected, precipitate itself "in a primordial form . . . in a fictional direction, which remains always irreducible."[14] Cardinality and calendarity provide the framework for such fetishes.

"Fight!": The final finality of the consumption of a herd-society

Contemporary global calendarity and cardinality, controlled by the cultural industries—not only television and radio but also the Internet and the integrated system of telecommunications, informatics, and the audiovisual, the product of the convergence of electronic technologies—form a system that functions according to a finality submitted to a calculation, that is, according to *a finished finality, one that is manifestly exhaustible.*

This system engenders herd behavior and not, contrary to legend, individual behavior. To say we live in an individualistic society is a patent lie, an extraordinarily false delusion, and, moreover, extraordinary because no one seems conscious of it, as if the efficacy of the lie was proportional to its enormity, and as if the lie was nobody's responsibility. We live in a herd-society, as comprehended and anticipated by Nietzsche. Some think this society individualistic because, at the very highest levels of public and private responsibility, but also in the smallest details of those processes of adoption stamped by marketing and the organization of consumption, egotism has been elevated to the pinnacle of life. But individualism has no relation to this egotism. Individualism wants the flourishing of the individual, this being always and indissociably a *we* and an *I*, an *I* in a *we* or a *we* composed of *I*s, incarnated by *I*s. To oppose the individual and the collective is to transform individuation into social atomization, producing a herd. The violence of which I spoke at the beginning—the violence of those one calls "little savages" [*"sauvageons"*],[15] for example—is kindled by today's hegemonic discourse, according to which life is the struggle for life, which is legitimated by the need to "get by through any means." "Fight!" is the maxim of such a point of view. This pseudo-individualist discourse, degraded and degrading—these are the males of the herd who attack each other—promotes ultra-egotistical behavior, which, combined with the loss of narcissism, that is, the loss of the understanding of limits, opens the door to all transgressions.

"The family" and ruin

The calendrical and cardinal system, insofar as, until now, it organized the memory of an immemorial event—a founding fiction, exceptional mirror of the absolute future, forming itself an absolute past that is necessarily mythic—was what permitted the commonality required for the constitution, precisely, of any accord. Calendarity opens commonality: *philia*, love, desire. As Vance Packard[16] clearly showed, cultural industries aim to produce such a commonality of desire by capturing and channeling the libidinal potential of consumers, who form audiences for advertisers mandated by producers of consumer objects. We arrive here at a totally integrated ensemble, where the symbolic and mnemotechnical system, calendrical and cardinal, combines with the technical system for the production of consumer goods, integrates with this system, and *submits to it*. All this is articulated in a single system where the organ of television is called to fuse with the organ of tele-action. In the end television will become an access terminal that will permit a viewer, while watching the program, to order a product, and this will in turn set in motion a "reassorting" (a resupplying of stocks), and, in setting this "reassortment" in motion, a command will also be issued for the production of the product, and so on. This tele-action terminal, which I can use at home to consume while watching television, will be found again in my business as a tool serving to direct, for example, a production line. On the map of the history of social structures, this evolution consists in the integration of the technical system of production with the mnemotechnical system sharing out calendarity and cardinality.

This integration constitutes a ruin of crossed narcissisms (aiming at the one in the other) of the *I* and of the *we*. This ruin consists in the organization of what I call hypersynchronization.[17] A calendar is a system of synchronization. It defines the rendezvous of the *we*. A rendezvous, in a synchrony of the *we*, makes possible, however, diachronic possibilities. On the other hand, the development of cultural industries leads to a hypersynchronization that eliminates diachronization and paradoxically engenders a hyperdiachronization—that is, a rupture with the symbolic milieu, a decoupling of individual and collective time, a de-composition of the diachronic and the synchronic. The destruction of modes of collective life means that, for example, an adolescent who returns to the family home at 7 p.m. eats from the fridge, that the father does the same at 8 p.m., and nobody eats with anyone else, the only meeting point being, eventually, the television news. What organizes calendarity is neither local, nor familial, nor national, nor religious—because it is no longer a *we*—rather, it is the great televisual consumption system, a system that, in Truffaut's *Fahrenheit 451* (based on Bradbury's novel) was called, indeed, "the family."

Now, here in the present, we see the arrival of political "reality-TV" programs, or programs of "political reality," where, precisely, a man of politics is invited to stay, beneath the gaze of the cameras, with a family:

> TF1 has announced, on Wednesday, 27 August, on the occasion of its press conference for the new season, the launch of a new program "*which would like to bring closer together the man of politics and the citizen.*" Provisionally baptized *36 Hours*, this program, hosted by Ruth Elkrief, wants to "*immerse a man of politics*" for close to two days in the private and professional everyday life of a French family. This show is produced by 2P2L, which had produced "The Eyes in the Blues," dedicated to the French football team of 1998.[18]

Deception

This hypersynchronization engenders a hyperdiachronization, insofar as hypersymbols (synchronization is operated through symbols) engender *hyperdiaboles*—dia-bolization, social atomization, a total disconnection. This happens because hypersynchronization provokes a loss of libido in relation to the system of synchronization. This loss of libido, this disenchantment, is shown in a paradoxical fashion in research undertaken into the relation between publics and their medias: "I don't believe it anymore. I watch TV but I hate it." This is how interviewees respond. If you ask people what they think of the programming on TF1, they respond in general that they don't like it, that Arte is better, yet they admit to watching TF1 anyway. Others say it's all bad, that Arte has become as bad as the others, and yet admit watching both Arte and the other channels.

As for these apparent paradoxes—symptoms of what I very generally call *ill-being* [mal-être]—analysts, experts, and commentators mostly fail to comprehend the main thing, even though the situation seems clear enough. For example, to follow what happens in the political landscape with the vote for the National Front, one must watch TF1. There's no choice. One doesn't want to watch this channel, but one has to. I don't want to say that TF1 is the cause of the National Front: it is the calendrical ensemble that constitutes the TV program industry—of which TF1 is in France the premier representative—and that forms a new system of organization of the *we*, the development of which is *deceptive*. And this deception is a *primary* and essential element of the vote for the National Front. Even if it is not the only one, it conditions *all* the others. The audiences produced by the cultural industries do not form a *we* that produces *philia*, that creates desire. This "we," if it exists, would on the contrary tend to produce hate and disgust, and above all self-disgust. Who has not at some time felt, after having sat in front of the television, the whole time thinking there must be something better to do, that *disgust with oneself*? This is the sense in which, if we can still say *we*, it is truly *by default*.[19]

The destruction of time

In analyzing hypersynchronization, and in denouncing its ravaging effects, one must not, nevertheless, *oppose* synchrony and diachrony—and this is a question of method. It is necessary to reason not by opposition but by composition. The terms I have employed—*I, we, diachrony, synchrony*—designate entities one must distinguish without opposing, and which are always in the process of composing. Language, for example, is a synchronic milieu (as Saussure taught us) in which there is diachrony. If I speak and you listen to me, it's because I am not in absolute synchrony with you; but if I can speak to you, it is because my diachrony *tends* to synchronize with you. Language is the articulation of the diachronic and the synchronic, that is, the composition of two tendencies that are also forces, a composition that produces a dynamic process. And a language dies when these tendencies decompose. What I call the "becoming-diabolical" of symbols is the result of such a decomposition.

We tend naturally to oppose things rather than to compose them. Well beyond this seemingly obvious natural inclination, however, there is also the industrial exploitation of time—through the cardinality and calendarity of the cultural industries—which tends *structurally and organically* to decompose the synchronic and diachronic, in the sense one intends for the word *decomposition* when it is a matter of necrosis. In other words, this industrial "calendarity" *destroys time.* Or, in other words, the industrial exploitation of time (the time of consciousness become a market) is entropic: it eliminates the difference between becoming and future [*devenir et avenir*]. This produces a profound ill-being, a disgust, symptom of a liquidation of desire—what I have called elsewhere "disbanding" [*"débandade"*].[20]

Industrial temporal objects

I try in a general way to reason in terms of tendencies, with reference to Bergson, Freud, and Nietzsche. One must not oppose synchrony and diachrony, for the same reasons that led Freud to propose that the pleasure principle is *constituted* by the principle of reality, which is, however, on first analysis, its "opposite." The pleasure principle knots and unknots itself in the principle of reality, and these verbs denote that what is at stake is a process. This process of the destruction of the synchronic and diachronic, that is, the de-composition of the *I* and the *we* (or the collapse of the *I* and the *we*) through consumption—that is, by the systematic exploitation of instruments for *fabricating the demand* for consumption—leads to an exhaustion of libidinal energy. When we watch television, we consume an economic good that belongs to the class of what Husserl called *temporal objects*—in this case *an industrial temporal object*. As a general rule, a *temporal object* is an object of time-consciousness, *the flow of which occurs simultaneously with the consciousness of which it is the object—because this consciousness itself flows*. This consciousness is itself *essentially* temporal: it *never ceases* to flow; it has, like all temporal objects, a *beginning* and an *end*, and, between this beginning and end, it is nothing but temporal *flux*. Now, when you who are consciousnesses watch a broadcast or a film, your time-consciousness passes *into* the broadcast or *into* the film, *adhering* to the temporal object that is the object of your consciousness. If it is a television broadcast (rather than a cassette in your VCR), the World Cup, for example, then hundreds of millions of people watch it at the same moment as you, and *you synchronize yourself with those consciousnesses*—you are in the *same time-consciousness*.

Now, this synchronization enters tendentially into opposition with all possible diachronization. *This* is how the decomposition of the synchronic and diachronic operates. It is necessary here to deepen the notion of the temporal object, to understand the specificity and force of industrial temporal objects and how they make possible a synchronization of minds, that is, the exhaustion of diachronicity and thereby of libidinal energy. With Husserl, then, I call an object "temporal" if its flow coincides with the flux of the consciousness of which it is an object, which is itself essentially a flux and only ever constitutes itself along the course of time *as* flow. The melody is paradigmatic. A temporal object is a *tissue of retentions and protentions*. Now, this protentional and retentional process also frames the temporality of consciousness generally, and temporal objects permit in one blow the modification of the process of consciousness and, up to a certain point, influence and even control this process. It is in music that these processes are best formalized (in its military or religious functions, for example).

In the "now" of a melody, in the present moment of a musical object that flows, the note that is present can only be a note, rather than merely a sound, insofar as it retains within itself *the preceding note*, which remains present—a preceding note *still present*, which itself retains the preceding one, which in turn retains the preceding one, and so on. One must not confuse this *primary retention belonging to the present* of *perception* with *secondary retention*, such as, for example, the melody I heard yesterday, which I can hear again *in imagination* by the play of memory, and which constitutes the *past* of my consciousness. One must not confuse, says Husserl, perception (primary retention) and imagination (secondary retention).

Before the invention of the phonograph, it was absolutely impossible to hear the *same* melody twice. Now, since the invention of the phonogram, which is itself what I call a *tertiary retention* (a prosthesis of exteriorized memory), the identical repetition of the same temporal object has become possible, and this permits a better comprehension of the retentional process. Because when the same temporal *object* is produced twice in a row, it engenders two different temporal *phenomena*, and this means that primary retentions vary from one phenomenon to the other. Retentions of the first audition, in becoming secondary, play a selecting role in the primary retentions of the second audition. This is true in general, but the tertiary retention—the phonogram—makes it obvious. On the other hand, *tertiarized temporal objects*—that is, objects either recorded or converted into a controllable and transmissible signal (such as phonograms, but also films, and radio and television broadcasts)—are materialized time, which overdetermines the relations between primary and secondary retentions in general, *thus*, in a certain sense, permitting their *control*.

These industrial temporal objects are increasingly today what give rhythm to and frame the flux of consciousness that we are.

Moreover, with the mutations of technology currently underway, we pass from an industrial level to what we might call the *hyperindustrial*, which integrates the world of culture and spirit in its totality at the heart of a vast techno-industrial system, where the tools for producing material goods and those for creating and diffusing symbols and other "spiritual nourishment" have become the same. And when the television antenna becomes a terminal of tele-action, it will not only permit the viewing of programs, but also make possible remote actions based on those programs, such as purchasing, production, and many other functions of the industrial global production/consumption system.

The standardization of secondary retentions as the reign of symbolic misery

When ten million people watch the same broadcast—the same audiovisual temporal object—they synchronize their flux. Of course, their criteria for selecting retentions vary, and, therefore, they do not perceive the same phenomenon: they don't all think the same thing about what they watch. But if it is true that *secondary retentions* form the *selection criteria in primary retentions*, then the fact that the same people watch the *same* programs every day necessarily leads each "consciousness" into sharing *more and more identical secondary retentions*, and thus to selecting the same primary retentions. They end up being so well synchronized that they have lost their *diachrony*, that is, their singularity, which is to say their liberty, which always means their liberty *to think*.

The de-composition of the synchronic and the diachronic is the de-composition of idiomaticity and of sign-making in general, of signi-fying insofar as it is the *non-insignificant*. The liquidation of primordial narcissism, leading to a loss of self-esteem (the self, losing its diachrony, can no longer inspire in itself the desire for self), authorizes all transgressions, insofar as it is also the liquidation of the *we* as such, which becomes a herdlike *they*, and which in turn produces the great political catastrophes of the twentieth century. The suffering of Richard Durn will have been above all that of *not*

having the power to signify. He writes in his diary that everything
seems insignificant to him, and that he himself cannot signify.[21]
He cannot participate in individuation, cannot individuate himself. To individuate is to exist, *ex-sistere*, to experience the *consistence* of individuation, that is, the *necessity* and the *convergence* of
that and of *those* who exist within the same process—a process that
fundamentally arranges, however, as projection of the future of the
we as one, difference and multiplicity. From that moment, Richard Durn had truly found what we must call a-significance—the
limit of significance, beyond insignificance and as an unbearable
limit—to the point where it leads to an act of massacre. Such is
the consequence of *symbolic misery*, to which the liquidation of
significance leads—and from which no one, in the end, escapes.
It weighs or hangs like a phantom over so many dinners, for example, during which there is no longer anything to say.

The loss of symbolic participation as the destruction of individuation and April 21, 2002, in France

Leroi-Gourhan developed the concept of loss of participation—
which is close to what I describe here as the *loss of individuation*,
which consists in the destruction of the capacity for narcissistic
projection, that is, of the libido—and which would reach its limit
in what he called the appearance of the *mega-ethnic*. Mega-ethnic-
ity and the disappearance of aesthetic participation (which corresponds to the phenomena of exteriorization and the specialization
of human symbolic faculties in the industrial system) are incom-
prehensible if separated: "Thus figuration appears . . . indissociable
from those social events that maintain ethnic continuity," that is
to say, from the psychic and collective individuation of the *we*,
insofar as it is a process through which the *I* individuates itself as
well, as we will see in the second chapter.

> From this aspect, the degree of figurative participation coheres with
> the group's techno-economic characteristics. Figurative specialization

and the separation between actors and spectators attain a maximum in the modern mass, where the majority of individuals are no longer required to play roles as social figures, but where all occasions for prestige have been reduced by television to a state of pure spectacle.[22]

Now, symbolic *creativity* is the condition of individuation as *circuit*, where individual memory (that is, psychic individuation, the singular point of idiomatic differentiation) comes back to collective memory (that is, to collective individuation, which is produced as the consistence of individual singularities). This is the condition by which collective individuation renovates itself and continues on, and it is this symbolic creativity that finds itself threatened by the horizon of the mega-ethnic, threatened in its essence by specialization:

> It is evident that human development is heading in the direction of mega-ethnicity—a global unit of measurement rather like the "mega-deaths" devised to express the destructive power of atomic weapons. We therefore might well ask ourselves what continuing means of escape the zoological flux will have at its disposal—for complete dehumanization would eventually become prejudicial to the efficacy of the social machine, and it must therefore be kept in a sufficiently "sapient" state. In other words, we may wonder whether yet another process of exteriorization—this time the exteriorization of social symbolism—might not be taking place. In fact the process is already so advanced that we can clearly see the direction it is taking. . . . The time is not far off when all our manufactured iron will be processed in a small number of centers by entirely automatic methods; this has already happened in the case of oil, where the diversity of products is not great enough to hamper the development. We can see the time coming when government will no longer have to call upon the uncertain services of artillery, and the megadeaths will instead be processed indirectly from electronic control panels. This is in fact already feasible.[23]

And this is indeed how the Gulf War will in effect have taken place. The automated management of production or destruction affects the present, as a process of exteriorization of symbolic exchange in general, even if, as Leroi-Gourhan says, in its most vital core it seems irreducible, that is, as the constitution and stabilization of the familial cell aimed at in the courtship display, thereby ensuring the reproduction of the species. This would still necessitate a direct aesthetic participation by individuals—insofar as their libido must pass into action in one way or another:

> As for the social sphere, modern audiovisual techniques, imperfect as they are, already provide a most convenient staging-post. The age we live in is still filled with survivals from the past. The city worker still goes out to watch a soccer game, catch a fish, or attend a parade, and still has a life of responsiveness, restricted it is true, but one that may stretch to taking part in the activities of a club. If we exclude the vital cycle, activities involving direct response are increasingly confined to adolescence and the pre-conjugal period, when direct participation is necessary to collective survival. Until we get to the stage already reached by the species of domestic animals that are best suited to productivity—the stage of artificial insemination—it would, for the time being, seem that a modicum of social aesthetics will continue to surround our years of social maturing. In insect societies, by the way, that is the only period when the reproductive minority shows some independence of behavior.[24]

It must be noted that this text was published in 1965, and that since then there have appeared technologies of procreation, with the first in vitro fertilization taking place in 1977. Just as sexual reproduction can now become *passive* (without recourse to the eminently complex aesthetic sequence which in the past preceded and followed it, but with all the potential for frustrations that this engenders) so too can the loss of aesthetic participation (be it intellective, such as I have described here as the setting to work of singular secondary retentions, or be they corporeal, carnal, or manual, such as in the analyses of Leroi-Gourhan) lead to a literally catastropic *insensibilization*:

> The loss of manual discovery, of the personal encounter between human and matter in the exercise of a craft, has closed one of the doors to individual aesthetic innovation. At a different level artistic popularization [*vulgarisation*] enables the masses to live passively on

the planet's cultural stock. But art will eventually go the same way as adventure, and Chinese paintings and Mayan sculptures will pall like the cowboys and the Zulus simply because a minimum of participation is necessary in order to feel. The problem of this modicum of the personal in art is as important to the future of *Homo sapiens* as that of the deterioration of human motor function.[25]

"A minimum of participation is necessary in order to feel," and the insensibilization resulting from the global organization of consumption, and the hypersynchronization in which it consists (as negation of all diachrony), produces immense suffering, to the *limit* of suffering, of what is bearable, an extraordinarily dangerous quasi-insensibility, an immiseration of sense, an impossibility of signi-fying, that is, of existing, which is the profound meaning of the vote of April 21, 2002, in France—but also of all desperate behavior in the world today, of which the murderer Richard Durn will have been one individual expression at the extreme of this loss of individuation.

§ 11   The destruction of the process of
        psychic and collective individuation
        and the question of evil

The *they* where there is no longer any witness

Cultural industries serve to create markets. Audiovisual temporal objects permit the diffusion and mass adoption of behavioral
models through which consumers adopt new products. Marx said
it already: capitalism is essentially the creation of needs. Today, this
industrial fabrication of behavior has become truly dangerous: it is
an entropic process, which raises questions of cultural ecology, as
Jeremy Rifkin[1] and Naomi Klein[2] have shown on other grounds.
And André Gorz recalled recently[3] that it was Freud's nephew, Edward Bernays, who invented marketing as the technology of the
phantasm—as Vance Packard already understood by 1950.[4]
    The industrial exploitation of the power of temporal objects will
end in the exhaustion of conscious *desire,* which is founded on singularity and narcissism as an image of an otherness of myself. Such
is disbanding—the coming slowdown of consumption, caused by
the consumer's disgust [*dégoût*]—which is the pure and simple *destruction of one's taste* [*goût*]. If I spend fifty-two minutes in front
of a television program, my consciousness has lived those fifty-two
minutes in the time of the temporal object. At the cinema I am
not in my chair—I am in the screen. My consciousness passes into
the temporal object. I interiorize all these times as secondary retentions I share with the other spectators. So what retentional criteria

does the television industry rely on when deciding what programs to produce? It is always the same marketing agencies that define standards: *The Loft* of television channel M6 immediately finds its homologue on TF1. This is why the diversification of offerings (which in itself is an interesting fact) barely affects the dominant tendency.

The criteria put forward by channels regarding the constraints of marketing are inevitably interiorized by the public. From the moment you adhere temporally to the same channel of information every day, "meeting" at the same time, you adopt the same history of events as everyone who watches these broadcasts—and with whom, without knowing it, and in a singularly strange way, you have "had a rendezvous." And that difference of analysis, which was originally your own in relation to these "neighbors" (because your past was not the same as theirs), finds itself, little by little, and in an asymptotic manner, reduced. Your past, the support of your negentropic singularity, slowly, progressively, but definitely and systematically, becomes the same conscious past as that of the viewing *they.* Your "analyses," originally different, tend to become identical or, in other words, tend to *cease to be an analysis.*

Normally, if I witness the occurrence of an event and you witness the same event, we see two different things in the one event. Take, for example, a traffic accident: somebody gets hurt, there are three additional witnesses, and finally there is the driver. The three witnesses give three different versions of events. Spontaneously, one might tend to think that the reason each has understood the causality of the event differently is because each one saw things from a different location. And this is no doubt partially true, but I think above all this difference of viewpoints leads rather to the conclusion that the witnesses each have their own past, and therefore do not witness in the same way—in the first place because *a past grounds expectations, forms horizons of expectation that are proper to the past and that receive events and render them sensible to those to whom they happen.* One sees on the basis of a competence, formed by memories and correlative expectations, retentions and protentions, a "competence" that enables a "performance" (to speak like certain linguists), for example, a given event that I have witnessed and that will be verbalized in the form of a police statement.

But if, little by little and asymptotically, everything that comes to consciousness is identical to what strikes my "neighbor's" consciousness, then there is simply *no longer any witness.* The *I* is confounded with the *we*: they disappear in the *they* where there is no longer any witness. Thus the television news can "virtualize" a Gulf War, such that there is no longer anyone to denounce the horror, which is nonetheless broadcast live. Such is the product of cultural industries. And this is true for other channels, even the ones you don't watch. The channels use the same sources and, increasingly, the same commentary. There is an entropic integration of the channels themselves, for reasons similar to those that lead to the asymptotic liquidation of the diachrony of the *I*s, of "consciousnesses." All this engenders what has been called "*pensée unique*"[5] in reference to the thought of "elites," but this is nothing but the reflection, at the level of supposed "elites," of a more global process whereby industrial synchronization tendentially suspends all diachronizing difference in the appropriation of what I watch on television.

Response—the cult object

When I go to mass, to the temple, the synagogue, or the mosque, the officiator addresses me as a singularity responsible for who I am. He tries to install me in my responsibility, to diachronize me. And, from that point of view, the cult poses *in principle* that we, insofar as we synchronize ourselves, are *good* and *amicable* people only insofar as we install our synchrony within a diachrony *of principle*, that is, those who can synchronize *in principle* are those who are *primordially diachronic*. And the very goal of a synchronizing rendezvous is to *intensify* diachrony, that is, responsibility—I speak here of the responsibility of a *response*. The word *responsibility* is doubtless cumbersome for qualifying all these religious cults, but I nonetheless believe that it is something like a response (which is also a musical form), such that a *respondent* in response—who must respond quite faithfully (beyond what is the case in Catholic liturgy)—is centrally at stake in all cults. This is what in Christianity will be called conscience: one has *a conscience*, one is *responsible for the other*, alone, absolutely alone *facing God.*

The global audience

Our "consciences/consciousnesses" [*"consciences"*] are bombarded mediatically by the cultural industries, whose newspapers are, within "the media," less and less differentiable—and the honor of the noble profession of the journalist will be measured in the future against the shadow of the capacity for one or another to *distinguish* themselves. So our consciousness is also "bombarded," insofar as it is the consciousness *of our body*, and insofar as our bodies consume. It is a matter, in view of realizing the *industrial economies of scale that mass markets make possible*, of synchronizing the *behavior* of these bodies, insofar as they are traversed by those consciousnesses forming an industrial material available for sale—which Thierry Gaudin has, for fifteen years now, referred to as "audiences." These audiences have a price: they constitute metamarkets. The market—for toothpaste, mobile phones, and optional extras on cars—passes through the metamarket of audiences. If you want to install a product on the market, the problem is not so much achieving good industrial productivity, nor having a truly innovative product, but rather having access to a market where you can augment your margins thanks to economies of scale. It is a matter of gaining ever-larger audiences, because in the current state of economic war, to amortize industrial investments one must aim at global markets, and that is why calendarity inexorably conforms to the systems of global synchronization. This is the historical meaning of the football World Cup,[6] one of the first truly global events, which has become over recent decades a typical event within the apparatus of consumption, all in the name of that ancient practice—preeminent with respect to the primordial narcissism of the *we*—that sports were in the past.

Narcissism, diachrony, and incommensurability

This becoming of calendarity (and the shipwrecked press that has allowed itself to be engulfed—those organs previously devoted to the constitution of public opinion but now submerged in the "mass audience" fabricated by marketing) thus engenders loss of desire insofar as *desire depends on primordial narcissism, and insofar as this in turn depends on primordial diachrony* (that is, in principle, the elementary tendency of the composition of time insofar as it is not reducible to becoming while nevertheless always having to reckon with it). I cannot love myself except insofar as I know myself to be absolutely singular, for without this knowledge I may be overcome by anguish and despair; I may attach myself to a herd. My time is absolutely unique, irreducible to the time of others. I would prefer also that, phantasmatically, my time be reducible to the time of others: I search originarily for the fusional element that I phantasmatically project in "oceanic"[7] feeling, as in rapturous love, where, "against all the evidence of the senses, lovers will uphold that I and You are one."[8] But this desire to rejoin an original fusional milieu is *founded* in my primordial narcissism, that is, in the *intimate knowledge* that I am singular, *that I am not* the other. I *am* nothing but de-synchronized in relation to the other—in diachrony, the condition of harmony, just as in music, where one needs (in the modern sense starting with counterpoint) several instruments or voices, or (in the Greek sense) several intervals forming a mode. Consumption, on the other hand, engenders an archi-synchronization in which *I* am not—where I am targeted no longer as an *I* but as a consumer, according to the viewpoint of Benjamin Franklin, for whom the best index of God, if not its representative, had become the dollar.[9]

It is necessary to respect everybody, even the lowest of the low, so long as a cent remains in his pocket: as a consumer he has a right to respect. It is, of course, starting not from consumption that Franklin proposes that "time is money," but rather from labor as the obligation to earn. His sermons make the pursuit of pecuniary interest a duty and, in a sense, the sole guarantor of God. But as earnings are not possible without exchange, that is, a market, the intensification without limit of earning (which is here the index of the infinity of God) implies the extension without limit of markets, that is, the wholly unlimited intensification of consumption. One can thus ask oneself if, in the world of Franklin, something or someone can exist and have value if it is not *measurable, commensurable, calculable, and capable of being added up, that is, synchronizable in totality.*

Now, God is reputedly essentially incommensurable and is, as such, the guarantor of the incommensurability of everybody in relation to each other. He is, otherwise put, the synchronic insofar as it *responds* to the diachronic.

Disgust and discredit

The system of synchronization put in place by the cultural industries (which aim at the adoption of consumer products through a system of integrated marketing) leads to de-diachronization, that is, to disbanding through the loss of love of self, and thus leads— through the loss of love, by all and of all, and hence the loss of all faith and all *credit*—to ruin, *here including in the pecuniary sense,* in the *generalized reign of disgust,* that is, of the diabolical.[10] All this makes possible the mad cow and all the phenomena of rejection of consumer products: these processes are the symptoms of a primordial suffering, if I may put it like this—a suffering of primordial narcissism—which leads to no longer wanting to consume, and thus to grabbing onto a certain number of alibis to justify this refusal to consume, alibis that correspond moreover to evident realities (the prion is not a phantasm). It concerns catastrophic phenomena in the strict sense: *in a single blow,* extremely dangerous rejection behavior proliferates, testifying to the fact that the unlimited exploitation of consumption engenders a refusal to consume that is itself unlimited (but in another relation to the unlimited, called the infinite).

To this rejection of and disgust for industrial society as consumer society corresponds the rejection of political discourse and representation, *forms that have never ceased to incorporate the facts* by renouncing the exigency of a difference between facts and norms, adapting their action and inaction to the constraints of the system—struggling, for example, against inflation by colluding with the marketing of mass distribution, and thus sinking into discredit.

The theater of individuation and the memories of man

Simondon, in *L'individuation psychique et collective,*[11] shows that for the *I* to individuate itself, my individuation must participate in the process of collective individuation, that is, in the individuation of a *we* where, insofar as I am an *I*, I have always already found myself inscribed. *I* do not exist other than in a group: *my* individuation is the individuation of my *group*—with which nevertheless I am not confounded, and, moreover, I may belong to several groups, which may be in disharmony.

This is what Jouvet says: "The same man can at the same time be a good father, a judge in court or commander of infantry, Catholic, Protestant, or atheist, all of these in a succession of personages, but it is not this that makes a person. It is impossible to draw the traits from each of these roles and put them all together. Are we in accord? There are within this person continuous ways of passing from infantry commander to communist or to the MRP,[12] and this in turn creates problems. This series of personages do not simply succeed one another, and even have conflicts between them. Perhaps the commander of infantry will have difficulties with the Catholic."[13]

I can thus endlessly adopt different personages, which may oppose one another, and thus I may be in opposition with myself. Now the possibility of such a multiple belonging, which intensifies the inadequation of the *I* to itself, lies in the fact of the default of origin, in primordial inadequation as originary default of the process of individuation. And this fact is itself the origin of the original adoptive situation of man, in which consists his technicity, that is, his originary articulation with the prosthesis (the technical object), which constitutes his primordial milieu as well as his default of origin.

Hominization, the appearance of the living being that we ourselves are—*we*, that is, "Man" (who disgusts god)[14]—is the appearance of a being constituted not by two memories (where Weismann identifies the *germ* and the *soma* as being the two sources of memory that constitute a living sexed being), but rather three, the third memory being that of the technical milieu essential to that living being. From Weismann to contemporary molecular biology, the living sexed being is constituted by two memories: species memory, which is replayed each time one has a fecund sexual life and which recombines chromosomes, thus remixing the genetic patrimony of the species (and each living being is a carrier of that memory), and the individual nervous memory of that living sexed being. Animals have an individual memory, which is what makes it possible for them to be trained: chimpanzees, poodles, but also annelids, sea snails, great pond snails; one can submit them to an apprenticeship, through the work of conditioning. There is a plasticity of individual animal memory, and the farther one heads toward the higher animals, the greater the plasticity. But from the annelids to the great apes—the great ape being an outer limit—the apprenticeship of the individual cannot be transmitted to the species. This is why acquired characteristics are not inheritable. The negentropic potential of the nonhuman life form relies on the structural impermeability between genetic memory—the *germ*—and somatic memory, that is, the nervous memory of the individual animal. The evolution of species through the contingent recombination of chromosomes—which is independent of the individual goals of each animal—is what produces the negentropic diversification of life.

Nevertheless, millions of years ago a life form appeared that, to guarantee its viability, needed to give itself prostheses. As Leroi-Gourhan says, it is naked, deprived of a viable natural defense system. And it surrounds itself with fabricated objects—with flint cutting tools, and then with the billions of objects of mass consumption produced by industrialization. In a certain manner, technological diversification has today become more important than biological diversification.

This is the appearance of the third memory, which I name epiphylogenetic. Genetic memory, which is transmitted from generation to generation, combines with the epigenetic memory of individual experience, which becomes transmissible through technical objects. This third memory is also that of the third person—that is, what we must name the *he*,[15] condition and bond of the *I* and the *we*. When I inherit an object, a flint cutting tool, for example, I inherit through it its mode of use, that is, the gestures, the motor behaviors that lead to the production of the flint cutting tool. With the appearance of technical objects, a new stratum of memory is constituted, which permits the transmission from generation to generation of individual experience and permits mutualization in the form of what we call a *we*. This permitted me to say to you earlier: "I, Bernard Stiegler, of German parents, am nonetheless French." This is only possible because I inherit traces of a *we*—for example, the *sans-culottes,* which form part of the fictive past of France—which I have appropriated, forming an artificial retentional milieu, a mnemotechnical milieu that I adopt and that permits me in this way to individuate myself in a *we* called "France." And today's question is to know how to fabricate the *we* of Europe. A provisional response, and one by default: certainly not by reproducing the American machine for the liquidation of the *we*.

This third memory, as the "third person," and as the *he*, is also the condition of the Book that speaks the *He*, that is, it is what sends us back to the absolute past, toward that which accumulated memory sends us as the utterly immemorial, as what Blanchot called the "awfully ancient," and which the Old Testament designates as "Eternal Father."[16] The Book, as third memory, is that which therefore supports the cult—with the rosary that, as Pascal notes, sustains faith. That is to say, also, credit.

Between the two world wars, and above all after the second, an important mutation is produced in the history of spirit, that is, in the history of epiphylogenesis, of the third person, of the *he*, and which is the "death of the He," which Hegel, Marx, and Nietzsche designate as the death of God: industry takes hold of that which becomes the premier metamaterial—*consciousness*. *Our* consciousnesses. Our *times of* consciousness.

It may seem paradoxical to suggest that consciousness is a primary material, since it is "on the side of" spirit and not the body. The epiphylogenetic character of human time, however, *directly* affects consciousness, which is the very reality of human *time*. Consciousness is materially overdetermined and originarily *constituted* by the fact that the flesh which incarnates and supports it is itself in movement—that is, moved—and supported by the process of exteriorization, the results of which I described as epiphylogenesis, that is, as the system of prosthetic supports of which the electronic technologies controlling time-consciousness are the most recent epoch. But, equally, consciousness is essentially memory (of the past), itself inscribed in imagination (of the future). Now, the epiphylogenetic stratum in which technical objects consist is a *material retentional milieu* that fundamentally affects retentional and protentional activity (that is, the phenomena of expectations, of protentions, engendered by retentions, by "memories") of consciousness.

This is why in the course of the twentieth century, with the appearance of mass media, which are retentional technologies, the mind can be targeted and *commercialized* as a *mode of access to the market*. "The market" is essentially a mass of consciousnesses, inhabiting the mass of consuming bodies. To launch a new toothpaste it is necessary to pass through these markets of time-consciousness that the mass media are. TF1 sells time-consciousness to advertisers, and the price is easily calculated. Consider the fact that an hour's worth of prime-time advertising on TF1 returns 500,000 euros. If the station attains an audience of fifteen million consciousnesses for one hour, the price of an hour of consciousness on that channel is approximately three cents. This is not expensive. When we watch TF1, our consciousness is not worth very much.

When America Online and Time Warner merge, it is to "get" consciousness at a "better price" on the global market. This industrial fusion, which is also that of program catalogues and data files of subscribers, has the goal of creating economies of scale, that is, "productivity gains," reaching daily not just dozens but hundreds of millions of consciousnesses. This operation may founder—the frenzy of speculators in this field has never been so great in industrial history. This mimetic madness nevertheless has causes which concern the very limits I am trying here to discern in the perenniality of the process.

When the mass media target consciousnesses insofar as they are metamarkets, spectators constitute a "primary material" for sale, the clients are the advertisers, and through them, industry tends to cause the adoption of behavior. The "primary material" is what one calls the audience, a mass of consciousnesses controlled by systems and processes for diffusing signals—that is, material states incorporated by the said "consciousnesses" (because the information is not "immaterial," it is a transitory material state)—and these consciousnesses are mental states engendering in their turn motor behaviors. When audiences of this kind are synchronized, they tend, asymptotically, to no longer constitute a *we* but rather a *they*. I don't want to say that when you (that is, *your consciousness*) watch television (and you necessarily watch it with others, at the same time as others), you are led immediately to think the same thing as others. I mean to say that television is a process that *tends* to make you conform progressively to an *average*. In that average[17] the difference between *I* and *we* is diluted, giving the *they*, that is, the loss of individuation of both the *I* and the *we*, at the heart of which alone can one individuate oneself.

The absorption of the *he*

Mnemotechnologies put to work by cultural industries are nothing but the industrial exploitation of the fact that memory is always artifactually produced. In the twentieth century, memory becomes the object of systematic industrial exploitation because markets become accessible through the metamarket of consciousness. This epiphylogenetic stratum constitutes the time of consciousness. It is the milieu common to all consciousnesses that industry wishes to grasp and exploit—it is this that is absolutely new. Until the nineteenth century there was a structural separation between the world of producers, entrepreneurs, those who produce material goods, and, on the other hand, those who, going by the name of "clerics"—ecclesiastical or lay—were in charge of religion, law, politics, knowledge, art, in essence the "spiritual." There were two separate worlds. With the integration of mnemotechnologies into the sphere of production—which tends to guarantee the synchronization of production and consumption, to minimize lead time, to make production work *"just in time"*[18]—these two worlds became fused: the *he*, the great third that constitutes authority as such, beyond the *I* and the *we*, has been integrated, has become immanent, that is to say, in principle, dia-bolical. All incommensurability—that transcendence which up until then had been expressed by the fact of the separation of the clerics—has been suppressed. This incommensurable third could also be called, if we want to speak the language of Lacan, the *big Other* (already in Aristotle the infinite cause of desire). With the absorption of this third, disbanding begins—which is also the reign of the in-significant, *such that it tends toward the a-significant.*[19]

If "God is dead," the "devil" is still alive and well. This is what *remains* for thought—as that which is contained in the remains, that is, in the traces of the *he* that has become, in its death, the primary material of consciousness commensurable on the market.

The combat of becoming and the future: Conjugating, disconnecting, inventing, excepting oneself

The integration of technical and mnemotechnical systems is a fact, a very long-term process that it would be deluded to "resist." Leroi-Gourhan summarizes this tendency with a concept that I have myself taken up: *exteriorization*. Nevertheless, this process opens alternative possibilities. It is not a blind determinism and, in that framework, questions of political economy are suggested that are still poorly identified, because of a failure to distinguish what is related to *becoming*, the process, and what is related to *time*, that which we *make* of the process. Now, this process requires that we make choices, that is, *differences*, there where it seems at first to consist, as mere becoming, in an elimination of general differences, what I call hypersynchronization. The production of differences cannot take place other than through a *critique of what in the process condemns the process itself*.

The pragmatic that I use to treat these questions consists in proposing that there are *conjunctions* and that, to intervene in the real, one must *take account of the conjunctivity of problems*. A problem is never purely technical: it is also legal, economic, sociological, psychological, and so on—to be brief, it is anthropological. Even if technics is *constitutive* of anthropology, and, in that sense, man is a prosthetic life form, he is nevertheless not *only* technical. If one day he becomes *entirely* technical, then he will no longer be called man—a transformation, moreover, perhaps already partly accomplished as the transformation of life in biotechnology. But then, for the process to continue, it would be necessary to find *another support for diachronicity and desire* other than man—thus the question remains.[20] This hypothesis notwithstanding, it is necessary to compose the problem of conjunctivity. Rather than thinking through *opposition*, it is preferable to proceed through *composition*. We must negotiate, because this conjunctivity is traversed by tendencies that concern what we call *becoming*. But negotiating does not mean renouncing or adapting. *It is a matter neither of adapting nor resisting*: it is a matter of *inventing*. And such invention is nothing other than combat, which is itself nothing other than *radical critique*.

Becoming is a *process* we never master. This is why contemporary philosophy denounces the Cartesian discourse of mastery. From the nineteenth century, at least from Nietzsche's time, modern thought begins to admit that one cannot master becoming. One can only negotiate with it, which is another thing entirely. Becoming is a movement that one must understand in order, eventually, to inscribe it in impulsions, that is, to operate *disjunctions*, on the condition, however, of not being able to control the effects. Reality is conjunctive, a complex movement where each one tries to "find one's place." Without us, this complex is nothing. So, *we* are the *dynamic inadequation* of this complex: *insofar as* we can say *we*, on the condition that we can say *we*, such that this *we* is precisely not a *they*, we stand, if not before or after this process, as least as that which *in* the process is at the same time its delay and its advance. As such, we *exceed* this process, we are even the *exception* that can unsettle the process—through disjunctions. This means that I *decide*, that I am capable, eventually, of *opposing myself* to this process, of temporarily "resisting," on condition that I do not reason by simple oppositions, and that, *composing with the process*, I am at the same time capable of putting it to work *through my capacity for invention*—and thus, well beyond my capacity for "resistance." I cannot resist by protesting: I must have intelligence about it, that is, be in excess of it, and by that same fact already be, in *advance*, inventive.

There are decisions to make: micro-decisions (for example, I buy toothpaste *X* rather than toothpaste *Y*) and macro-decisions (I vote for a candidate for the presidency of the Republic or decide to press a red button to destroy a population with atomic weapons—or I send an armed force to Iraq). Some are very small, while others are enormous, inconceivable. But there are always choices to make. Time is the question of that choice, of deliberation and action.

The question of evil and the thought of tendencies

For someone who does not know how to reason in terms of tendencies, the question of evil is a dangerous question, a bad question—it is in a certain sense the evil itself, the menacing question or the question that Nietzsche considers to be the villain. To think in terms of tendencies is to think that *that against which one fights is necessary*. That is, if one fights against a tendency, insofar as that tendency tends to become hegemonic (and in fact all tendencies tend toward hegemony against another hegemony), and if one opposes there a countertendency, one must know that *the tendency against which one fights is the condition of the tendency for which one fights*. Consequently, it is not a matter of eliminating the tendency being combated but of *composing* tendencies. From this point of view, thinking through tendencies excludes seeing in the adversary an enemy who is the *cause* of evil. The adversary is not an enemy who is the cause of evil—in other words he is not the evil—but is caught in a hegemonic tendency of which he has become the vector, the spokesperson, most of the time without having any impression of harboring bad intentions.

The obvious difficulty of such a manner of thinking and acting is that it seems to take one back to the discourse of the golden mean. Not that of Aristotle's ethics but, in modern language, the discourse of reformism and adaptation, the discourse that systematically ignores radical questions (which are the only true questions, those that produce major improvements, as Simondon says, while the minor improvements of the reformists hide the necessity for "quantum leaps" in that becoming which individuation is).

In reality, nothing is more radical than a critique that prohibits itself from diabolizing the adversary or the tendency—because the counterpart of the thought of the process as the irreducibility of one tendency to another is the thought that what permits the (re)com-position of tendencies in the process of individuation is the *exception*: that which is neither the average, nor adaptation, nor the mass, nor consensus. This is what puts dissensus, getting out of phase [*déphasage*], and disadjustment—what the ancient Greeks named *eris*— at the very heart of becoming (such is the Simondonian theory of quantum leaps) and as its very possibility. It is the spirit of this *eris*, which designates emulation and competition, that the organization of consumption degrades in the commensurability of all diachronies, that is, in total calculability in the service of the greatest possible and most immediate profit, that is, in the service of "*just in time,*" and the reactivity that inclines the tendency toward hypersynchronization.

A building site

These are the networks of communication and information that diffuse industrial temporal objects and constitute the infrastructure of hypersynchronization, which decomposes the social fabric and exhausts desire in opposing synchronization and diachronization, by rendering the diachronization of consciousnesses impossible through the control of mass retentional processes.

A mutation has been produced in the world of networks since 1992, with the appearance of the Internet. This network of networks, unified by the TCP-IP protocol, has manifestly changed the organizational setup of the program industries. And there is no doubt that this transformation of industrial technology, via the digital, renders new perspectives conceivable. These must be systematically explored; they constitute a privileged terrain of combat and a field for social invention that could be extremely fertile. I believe more than anything else in the necessity of acting in this domain.[21]

For so many, the critique that must accompany invention, if this is even possible—and, I repeat, it is only possible as combat, at the same time economic, geopolitical, and ecological (it is a matter of an ecology of the milieus of spirit)—this critique must analyze in every detail the manner in which the rupture that makes imaginable and possible a technological mutation of the digital (as the possibility for demassifying the diffusion of information and industrial temporal objects) has already been invested in and controlled by the industrial retentional system placed into the service of consumption and hypersynchronization, and is still reinforcing it, contrary to appearances.

The question of the network, as Jeremy Rifkin has shown well, is *access.* What is important is the *filters.* The search engines that permit the ranking of information charge those whom they reference. This is always a question of selection. The Google search engine, for example, is a system that requires the "people meter" [*audimat*]: it proposes to you that which has been most in demand, thus systematically reinforcing social mimetism and herdish behavior. Another access and navigation technique, *user profiling*,[22] consists in identifying your search behavior in order to propose something to you before you even have the idea of asking for it. If this is not a *programming* of consciousness, it is *conditioning* and *reinforcement,* in the Pavlovian sense of these terms. You are locked into your synchronicity, prevented from changing, and, through this, what is pursued amounts to hypersegmentation, a marketing strategy for identifying ultraprecise niches. This is how behavior is standardized, reduced to socio-professional categories or "tribes," identifiable through "markers" that are much more interesting to marketing than is political society.

The media deploy industrial technology for the exploitation of consciousness, and do so through the imposition of retentional *criteria*. This control of retentional systems where consciousness is a market, where an hour of consciousness is worth the sum of the advertising receipts divided by the number of viewers, has the effect of homogenizing secondary retention. And this is an essential cause (if not the only cause) of what I call ill-being. The control of retention implies the loss of identity, that is, of difference. Nietzsche saw very clearly this lost capacity to produce a difference and the tendency of societies falsely named "individualistic" to deny the exception. Our supposedly individualistic societies are in reality perfectly conformist.

Singularity in the process of individuation

What Simondon called the *trans-individual* is constituted by the epiphylogenetic domain of technical objects that I inherit. Individuation is not individualization. Individualization is the result of individuation. This is the manner in which the diverse in general unifies itself asymptotically in an indivisible way. I *tend* to become indivisible—but I never get there. I tend to become myself—"me" as indivisible, as pure unity—but I never get there, because processes of individuation are never finished. Or, when they are finished, they have not reached their goal: having ended, they have run aground. A process of individuation is that which *structurally cannot* be completed . . . unless it *carries on through a process of transmission*, through which this *I* that individuates itself, and which has come to the end of its individuation—it is dead—may eventually become a source for a new process of individuation for its descendants: for *we* who inherit from this *I* that individuated itself by default, that came to its finish by default.

In other words, every process of individuation is dynamic, to the degree that it is always *inadequate* to itself—*which is the inscription of its diachrony in its synchrony*. I aim to individuate myself, to become indivisible, but in the asymptotic quest for my indivisibility, I *alter myself*, I reveal myself as other, because I am inhabited by an inadequation that is my diachrony. I am always out of phase with myself: I am never in a pure present. I can only attain the pure present when I am dead—but upon dying I will no longer be there, and thus I will never succeed in individuating myself properly speaking. Being dead, however, I can become an ancestor who leaves traces, objects, works—where by "works" I do not mean my "complete works" but rather perhaps the library I bought, the garden I cultivated, all sorts of things: those objects in which, or the phrases, acts, or gestures by which, *in one way or another*, something of my singularity is inscribed—"something of my singularity" meaning *my inadequation with myself, that is, with the group*. Insofar as I belong to a group, I am, within the group, a singularity that nourishes the group in alterity.

Milieus of the *we*

A process of individuation always puts in play a tension harboring a potential. Individuation is the syn-crystallization of a mother liquid, of a potential that can catalyze, crystallize, take the form of a crystal, with the qualification that psychic and collective individuation (of the *I* in the *we*) is a syn-crystallization that *structurally* fails, whereas a crystal succeeds in congealing completely. Life is a crystal that does not reach crystallization, caught in a process of *metastable equilibrium*. The potential of the *I* and the *we* is the legacy of this metastability (equilibrium at the limit of disequilibrium) that I inherit through traces. These traces are the monuments of the dead, the library that is here behind bars, the chateau at Cerisy with its phantoms, all these memories.[23] It is also TF1. It is everything transmitted to me that is memorable. And these memories I share with others—more or less. Obviously, if I was a practicing Jew in Israel, I would not share the space of Jerusalem with practicing Muslims in the same way as would another Muslim. There are conflicts over sharing, over heritage. There are localizations in the capacities for appropriating the preindividual potential that open common scenes of individuation forming precisely the *we*.

The epiphylogenetic preindividual milieu is the theater of individuation of which Simondon speaks.[24] And thus individuation has a history: one does not individuate oneself in the Australopithicus epoch in the same way as in the Cro-Magnon epoch, as Greek citizens or during the industrial revolution. And the *they* does not individuate itself today—in the *hyperindustrial* epoch—as during the industrial revolution: the epiphylogenetic milieu has been transformed, and the conditions of individuation are transformed by the evolution of technics.

The chance of a *we*

Nevertheless, for the *I* to individuate itself, it is necessary that my individuation take part in the individuation of a *we* to which I belong—and which has a part *in* this individuation. At this moment, as I am speaking to you, I am in the process of individuating myself. I propose a new argument, even if it is not *completely* new—I have already spoken of these things in this very place.[25] But at that time, April 21 had not yet taken place. Now that it has taken place, I reread my proper preindividual ground, and I reindividuate, at the very moment that I speak to you: individuating myself means seeking to constitute the symbolic coherence of my discourse. But I will only succeed in individuating myself tendentially (to reinforce my "potential" for individuation*) if I succeed in making you individuate yourselves with me.* If my individuation succeeds, it will have to have succeeded in you—but not at all in the same manner, because what I am in the process of telling you *I hear and interpret one way while you hear it ANOTHER way,* and this is why in a moment we could perhaps have a debate, which *we hope will be fecund*—this is the *condition of a we.* Because in my discourse something is still inadequate, remains to come, is open to the future, and this is the object of our discussion. Only here can there be the chance for a *we*: that we might understand each other, in spite of this inadequation and because of it—in this fact lies the possibility and necessity of affirming that, yes, the future lies in this very inadequation itself.

Colloquium at Cerisy: Metastability

Cerisy is a group. The goal of a decade at Cerisy is to give ourselves the means, through an appropriate calendarity, for the mobilization of a preindividual ground, which we share in psychically and collectively individuating through conferences to form such a group. It is a metastable process precisely in that it is not stable: if it was, it would be a totally ossified crystal, without future or temporality; if it was totally unstable, it would lead to an explosion of the group—atomization, pulverization, entropy, absolute disequilibrium. A group is always between equilibrium and disequilibrium, neither in equilibrium nor in disequilibrium, but rather always at the border of both: at the border of pure equilibrium, which is called pure synchrony, the crystal being purely synchronic; and of disequilibrium, that is, of pure diachrony, total atomization, completed *diabelein.* Disequilibrium exists in groups, and it is called madness. Madness is *at the heart* of the process of individuation: it is the energy itself of individuation, but it is an energy that must be, precisely, *calendarized and cardinalized* to be channeled and to form something that creates movement without leading to disintegration. Metastability produces movement.

Pure disequilibrium is the collapse of movement. Pure equilibrium is immobility preceding movement. Between these two is fragile metastability. Calendar and cardinal systems are the stabilizers that serve to create the metastatic—the technics of space and of time. One can analyze these in a precise and historical way: hence the emergence of the Egyptian calendar from its conditions of appearance, linked to the conditions of the flooding of the Nile, primitive accumulation, things well understood by archaeologists. These are the technical concretions of the relation to space and time through calendar and cardinal systems, which permit the metastabilization of the potential for madness that the group always contains.

Das Man

Calendarity, for millennia, has meant that I have the feeling of belonging to a *we*, because I share with others, with other *Is*, a common calendar, which refers to moments of prayer, festival, singing, fetishes in general, moments of concelebration, which are not necessarily religious—and fetishes that will lead to both Marxian and Freudian fetishism (Marx conceived of commodities *essentially* as fetishes). When they are integrated in an epiphylogenetic industrial system—where there is no longer any distinction between the spiritual world of the clerics and the world of production in the new world of consumption—the calendrical and cardinal systems lose their efficacy. When I watch the television news each day at the same time with around fifteen million people in France, a synchronization of the *I* is produced that is no longer the care of an *I* or of an ensemble of *Is* in the interior of a *we*, but the confusion of the *Is* and the *we*: totalitarianism as the elimination of the differences of the *I* and the *we*, in what a German has called "*das Man*," the *they*—he himself fell into this *they*. Six years after having announced the danger of *das Man* he wore the swastika. I point this out not to condemn the memory of Heidegger (the heritage and inadequations of which are at the heart of all of these questions) but to remind us of a certain prudence and modesty:

it is not by denouncing the *they* that one avoids the risk of falling into it, and perhaps the opposite is true, as is often seen in times of great reactivity.

Collapses: September 11, March 26, April 21

The commodification of consciousness is essentially synchronic, whereas you listen to me because I am a diachronic consciousness—and I can only speak to you because you are diachronic consciousnesses. You only listen to me because you think I have something to tell you. You don't know it: you hope that I am in structural diachrony in relation to you (hoping that I thus promise a synchrony to come—but to *the infinite*). And if I speak to you, it is because I think I have something to tell you. But at the same time, I can only speak to you because I think that a synchrony between us is possible, for otherwise I would say nothing to you. I argue that this diachronic tension—which is the condition of the individuation of a *we*, that is, of a synchrony that remains always to come, this inadequation between *I* and *we* that is the condition of the existence of the *I* and the *we*—in the present epiphylogenetic epoch, that is, in the epoch of the industrial exploitation of mnemotechnical supports, collapses. From then on, absolute atomization and suicidal behavior is produced—such as that of April 21, Osama bin Laden, Richard Durn, George W. Bush, or other forms of toxicomania.

The spirit consists in states of matter, whether it be the flint cutting tool at the beginning of hominization or material states at the order of the pico-second, when it concerns information. Information is not immaterial but is rather a flux of material states, which circulate extremely quickly, bombarding our consciousness and conditioning our mental states. If we do not enact an *ecological critique* of the technologies and the industries of the spirit, if we do not show that the unlimited exploitation of spirits as markets leads to a ruin comparable to that which the Soviet Union and the great capitalist countries have been able to create by exploiting territories or natural resources without any care to preserve their hab-

itability to come—the future—then we move ineluctably toward a
global social explosion, that is, toward absolute war.

The "diabolical," critique, invention, and combat

We spoke already of these questions and these threats a year
ago, just after September 11, here at Cerisy. Since then, April 21
has taken place, that is, the problem has come into greater focus.
I fear that all this is merely the beginning of a long and arduous
path. On this path one must cast all doubt aside to fight the im-
minent possibility of the total atomization of the *we*. This path
passes through a critique of what spirit is today, and thus through
an analysis of the conditions in which metastability can again become metastable, that is, not fall into equilibrium or disequilibrium—which is the same thing: pure equilibrium creates absolute
disequilibrium—but rather produce new *movement*. Pure equilibrium is the loss of desire that creates atomization. Hypersynchronization creates hyperdiachronization, that is, the decomposition
of the social. Such is the veritable "diabolical" that is masked by
the demonizing [*diabolisation*] of supposedly rogue states supposedly linked to an "axis of evil."

What more than anything is *evil* is *OUR renunciation of thought
in favor of the denunciation of evil*. What is evil is the *we*, disquieted
about the future of the *we*, that renounces *critique* and *invention*
or, in other words, *combat*.

Notes

How I Became a Philosopher

1. This text was delivered on April 23, 2003, at the Centre Georges-Pompidou, at the invitation of Marianne Alphant, whom I thank, in the context of the "Les Revues Parlées" lecture series. The topic was: "Philosophers reflect on their path: Why and how has one come to philosophy? Why does one become a philosopher? Why does one remain a philosopher? This series, which proposes to reinscribe the philosophical project in the intimacy and secret of a life, can touch on themes sometimes outside of the philosophical 'mode'—such as God, Being, Humanism, What is thought?—considered from a perspective that sees the defense of philosophy as one of the urgent contemporary civic principles."

2. Catherine Clément, "Vocation," article in *Encyclopaedia Universalis*.

3. Even if this "just as much as" is not an "as"; on this point, cf. Stiegler, *La Technique et le Temps, 3. Le temps du cinéma et la question du mal-être* (Paris: Galilée, 2001), p. 147.

4. Gilbert Simondon, *L'Individuation psychique et collective* (Paris: Aubier-Montaigne, 1989), p. 11.

5. Plato, *Crito* 53e.

6. J. L. Austin, *How to Do Things with Words* (Oxford: Oxford University Press, 1962).

7. Maurice Blanchot, *The Infinite Conversation* (Minneapolis: University of Minnesota Press, 1993), pp. 11–12.

8. They are found not in experience but rather in *extraordinary experiences* and *at the limit of the social*—as that which delimits the social, practices that *suspend the ordinary*—whether these are experiences of religious life, of thought, of painting (such is the extra-ordinariness of Mont

Sainte-Victoire), of listening, of dance, of writing, music, literature, and so on, each forming as many modalities of flight beyond the element.

9. Which finds the possibility of the world constituted by the transcendental ego, that is, by the constituting subjectivity.

10. Because I will propose that the hypomnesic supplementarity of the world is constitutive, and that this world, as accidental facticity, is therefore irreducible.

11. Stéphane Mallarmé, *Oeuvres completes*, ed. Henri Mondor & G. Jean-Aubry (Paris: Gallimard, 1945), p. 368.

12. Stéphane Mallarmé, *Collected Poems*, trans. Henry Weinfield (Berkeley: University of California Press, 1994), p. 84; the original is in Mallarmé, *Oeuvres completes*, p. 76.

13. I develop this concept, in relation to the Husserlian concepts of primary and secondary retention, in *Technics and Time, 1: The Fault of Epimetheus* (Stanford, CA: Stanford University Press, 1998), part 2, ch. 3; *La Technique et le Temps, 2. La désorientation* (Paris: Galilée, 1996), ch. 4; and *La Technique et le Temps, 3*, chs. 1–2.

14. The difference between significant and insignificant is the concrete but always changing reality of great differences that take place in the history of thought, of which the most recent, formulated by Heidegger, is the difference between being and beings—which never ceases to be forgotten as we tend always to reduce the significant to the insignificant, a reduction toward which our *terrible idleness* does not cease to seduce us.

15. Stiegler, *La Technique et le Temps, 3*.

To Love, to Love Me, to Love Us, Part I

1. This book takes up and develops the text of a lecture delivered at Cerisy-la-Salle, at the invitation of Edith Heuregon and Josée Landrieu, at the opening of the colloquium "Of the I and the We: Working Together in the City. Prospective IV," on June 9, 2002.

2. On March 26, 2002, Richard Durn murdered eight members of the Nanterre city council. He committed suicide on March 28, 2002. The crime of Lance Corporal Lortie in Canada immediately springs to mind, which Pierre Legendre analyzed in *Le crime du caporal Lortie: Traité sur le père* (Paris: Fayard, 1989).

3. *Le Monde*, April 10, 2002.

4. On this matter, and from another viewpoint, Michel Schneider speaks of Durn's "narcissism of death" in *Esprit*, May 2002, and *Le*

Monde, November 12, 2002. Vincent de Gaulejac also gave a very interesting presentation analyzing Durn's passage to the act during the colloquium "L'Individu Hypermoderne," September 8, 2003, at the Ecole Supérieure de Commerce in Paris.

5. Sigmund Freud, "Psychoanalysis," *The Standard Edition of the Complete Psychological Works of Sigmund Freud*, ed. James Strachey, vol. 18 (London: Hogarth Press, 1955), p. 249, translation modified.

6. I have developed this concept of the *they* in *La Technique et le Temps, 3*, p. 156.

7. Ibid., p. 138. The process of adoption is consubstantial with the process of individuation.

8. An economy of scale permits, through the production of a series of the same object, the reduction of production costs. Thus a prototype automobile costing a million euros to make can see its price in the market reduced to 20,000 euros through economies of scale. But this presumes the constitution, for this product, of a market of global dimensions and the organization of consumption through pressure applied to the entire world's consumers, whose modes of life are therefore, through this object, synchronized.

9. This is what I examined in the first two chapters of *Technics and Time, 1*.

10. This is because human time exceeds the process of negative entropy by which Schrödinger and Brillouin characterized the living, by inscribing negentropy *outside* of this living, and as characteristic of the human's vital milieu and what I call its epiphylogenetic memory in *Technics and Time, 1*, pp. 139–40, 175–77.

11. Ernest Renan, "What Is a Nation?" in *The Poetry of the Celtic Races, and Other Studies*, trans. William G. Hutchison (London: Walter Scott, 1896), pp. 61-83.

12. François Ascher & Francis Godard (dir.), *L'Aube* (2003).

13. Aristotle, *Nicomachean Ethics*. See the translation by Jean Lauxerois of books VIII and IX, entitled *L'amicalité*, and his epilogue, "A titre amical" (Paris: A Propos, 2002), which concerns, writes Jean Lauxerois, "thinking today the default as bond of self to self and as the site of all possible community" (p. 88). Now, this default is that which *makes mistakes* in the *fictional* character of the self as much as of the community—producing *so many histories*. The default is what modern philosophy does not know how to think, and Lauxerois demonstrates this also in his translation of Sophocles' *Oedipus the Tyrant*, and in "Le pied de la

lettre," his magnificent epilogue (Paris: A Propos, 2001). I myself have for a long time explored this question of default, which will be the title of *La Technique et le Temps, 5. Le défaut qu'il faut* [The necessary default]. Now, Lauxerois seems to suggest that the *inability to cope with* the default leads to narcissism (pp. 90–91). He thinks narcissism according to the habitual notions that take it as pathological. For all that, what I am trying to suggest here is that primordial narcissism *is precisely the default* that we must think—beneath (on this side of) and beyond the "petit narcissism" of "petites différences," which is the subject of pages 118–20 of *L'amicalité*.

14. Jacques Lacan, "The Mirror Stage as Formative of the Function of the I as Revealed in Psychoanalytic Experience," *Ecrits: A Selection* (New York: W. W. Norton, 1977), p. 2.

15. *Translators' note.* The literal definition of *sauvageon* is a child who will not submit to any kind of discipline, but it is also a word that has been taken up in French political discourse. It has been used, for instance, by the French minister of the interior, Jean-Pierre Chevènement, and is an expression typical of a certain leftist populism, a populism tending to attribute individual, psychological, if not racial, characteristics to behavioral problems.

16. Vance Packard, *The Hidden Persuaders* (New York: David McKay, 1957).

17. Cf. *La Technique et le Temps, 3.*

18. *Le Monde*, August 29, 2003.

19. And the question is then to think the *default of origin* that constitutes the *we*: such is the constant intention of the five volumes (of which two are yet to appear) of *Technics and Time.* See note 13 above (on Aristotle) and *Comme si nous faisons défaut* [As if we were lacking], forthcoming from Éditions Galilée.

20. See Bernard Stiegler, *La mécréance et discrédit 1. La décadence des démocraties industrielles* (Paris: Galilée, 2004), p. 87. Translator's footnote: Literally, *débandade* means the disbanding of a group that results when it loses its unity and its members drift apart. Disbanding captures Stiegler's reference here to his discussion of the breakdown of the dynamic of individual and collective individuation. The characterization of this *débandade* as a "symptom of a liquidation of desire" is elaborated in relation to Freud's notion of libidinal energy in the following section.

21. On the question of the significant and the insignificant, permit me to refer to pp. 26–28 of this volume.

22. André Leroi-Gourhan, *Gesture and Speech* (Cambridge, MA: MIT Press, 1993), p. 356, translation modified.
23. Ibid., p. 358.
24. Ibid.
25. Ibid., p. 397.

To Love, to Love Me, to Love Us, Part II

1. Jeremy Rifkin, *The Age of Access: The New Culture of Hypercapitalism Where All Life Is a Paid-For Experience* (New York: G. P. Putnam, 2000).
2. Naomi Klein, *No Logo* (London: Flamingo, 2000).
3. André Gorz, *L'immatériel: Connaissance, valeur et capital* (Paris: Galilée, 2003), p. 64 and following.
4. Vance Packard, *The Hidden Persuaders*.
5. *Translators' note. Pensée unique* is a French term developed as part of a critique of certain political tendencies in France and elsewhere. It refers to the convergence of mainstream political discourse around what is broadly referred to as neoliberalism and to the feeling that there is in fact less and less difference to be found between ostensibly "opposed" political parties.
6. The World Cup was created in 1930 with an essentially sporting goal in mind. But it has become, with television, an essential vector of global calendarity in the service of consumption. The annual global turnover from football today is 200 billion euros.
7. Cf. Freud, *Civilization and Its Discontents*, in *Standard Edition*, vol. 21, p. 64. Freud cites someone who responds by letter to his book on religion as an illusion, agreeing with the judgment but offering his own account of the true source of religious sentiment: "This, he says, consists in a peculiar feeling, which he himself is never without, which he finds confirmed by many others, and which he may suppose is present in millions of people. It is a feeling which he would like to call a sensation of 'eternity,' a feeling as of something limitless, unbounded—as it were, 'oceanic.' This feeling, he adds, is a purely subjective fact, not an article of faith; it brings with it no assurance of personal immortality, but it is the source of the religious energy which is seized upon by the various Churches and religious systems, directed by them into particular channels, and doubtless also exhausted by them. One may, he thinks, rightly

call oneself religious on the ground of this oceanic feeling alone, even if one rejects every belief and every illusion."

8. Ibid., p. 66, translation modified.

9. Cf. Max Weber, *The Protestant Ethic and the Spirit of Capitalism* (London: George Allen & Unwin, 1930), pp. 48–50.

10. And in this regard one must reflect on the remark of Pope John Paul II: "God does not reveal much, seeming to hide in his heaven, in silence, seemingly disgusted by the actions of humanity." Cf. Massimo Cacciari, *La Republica,* December 12, 2002. I thank Patrick Talbot for having brought this article to my attention.

11. Gilbert Simondon, *L'individuation psychique et collective.*

12. *Translators' note.* The Mouvement Républicain Populaire, a defunct French political party.

13. Louis Jouvet, "Cours au Conservatoire National d'Art Dramatique, 1949–1951," *Revue de la Société d'Histoire du Théâtre.*

14. See above, note 10.

15. *Translators' note.* What is being translated here as "the *he*" is, in French, "*le* il," which of course could also be translated as "the *it*," and thus contains a reference to the artifactual, prosthetic, or technical basis of what Stiegler calls the "third" (person). If we prefer to retain the sense of the masculine rather than the artifactual in this translation, this is because the text elaborates on this "third" in terms of God and of Lacan's symbolic order (also termed by Lacan "the name of the father"), the masculinity of which Stiegler is referring to in what follows. Of course, both senses are important to Stiegler, and it is the relation between them that he is attempting to think.

16. On the *il,* the *he,* cf. Maurice Blanchot, *The Infinite Conversation* (Minneapolis: University of Minnesota Press, 1993), p. 71; on the "awfully ancient," cf. Blanchot, *The Space of Literature* (Lincoln: University of Nebraska Press, 1982), p. 229.

17. On the hegemony of the average, one can read with profit Gilles Châtelet, *Vivre et penser comme des porcs* (Paris: Exils, 1998).

18. In English in the original.

19. I distinguish between in-significance and a-significance above, pp. 26–30, and in *La Technique et le Temps, 4. Symboles et diaboles, ou la guerre des esprits,* forthcoming from Éditions Galilée.

20. I outlined this in "Ce qui fait défaut," *Césure* (September 1995).

21. I personally explored these questions as well when I was director of the Institut National de l'Audiovisuel (INA) and at the University

of Compiègne, and continued to do so at the Institut de Recherche et Coordination Acoustique/Musique (IRCAM). See notably "La numérisation des objets temporels," in *Cinéma et dernières technologies* (INA/De Boeck University, 1998); and "Sociétés d'auteurs et sémantiques situées," in Christian Jacob (dir.), *Des Alexandries* 2 (BNF, 2003).

22. In English in the original.

23. The lecture on which this text was based was delivered in the library at the chateau of Cerisy-la-Salle.

24. Simondon did not himself propose this epiphylogenetic dimension of the preindividual of psychic and collective individuation. On this question, see also Bernard Stiegler, "Technique et individuation dans l'oeuvre de Simondon," *Futur Antérieur* (Spring 1994); reprised in another version under the title "Temps, technique et individuation dans la pensée de Simondon," *Intellectica* (1999).

25. In September 2001, here in Cerisy, in the colloquium "Modernity: The New Map of the Times," under the direction of François Ascher and Francis Godard.

Index

accidentality, 10–12, 16, 22, 24–25,
  30, 33, 35
adoption, 41, 44–45, 48, 60–61,
  65–68, 70, 85n.7
Alphant, Marianne, 1, 10–11, 33,
  83n.1
anamnesis, 10, 15, 18, 23–24, 31, 34
Anytus, 3
Aristotle, 3, 13–14, 23, 47, 71, 74
artifact, 14, 26
asceticism, 19, 21
Austin, J. L., 6

Barthes, Roland, 31
Bergson, Henri, 52
Bernays, Edward, 60
bin Laden, Osama, 81
Blanchot, Maurice, 7–8, 21, 68
Bradbury, Ray, 50
Brillouin, Léon, 85n.10
Bush, George W., 81

calendarity, 45–46, 48–52, 63–64,
  79–80
cardinality, 45–46, 48–49, 52, 80
Char, René, 21
Chevènement, Jean-Pierre, 86n.15

Clément, Catherine, 1
composition, 52, 72–74
consistence, 32, 56–57
consumption, 41–46, 48–50, 53, 59–
  60, 63–65, 71, 74–75, 80, 85n.8
Crito, 5, 24
culture, 20, 43, 55

default, 4, 11–12, 14, 16–18, 21,
  23–24, 26, 30–31, 35, 47, 51, 66,
  77, 85n.13
Derrida, Jacques, 23, 28, 31
desire, 7–8, 32, 47, 49, 51–52, 60,
  64, 75, 82
Diotima, 8
disadjustment, 42, 74
disbanding, 52, 65, 71, 86n.20
Durn, Richard, 39–40, 55–56, 59,
  81, 84n.2, 84n.4

Epictetus, 20
Epimetheus, 16
epiphylogenesis, 68–69, 71, 76, 78,
  80, 85n.10, 89n.24
epokhe, 22, 29
evil, 73–74, 82
extraordinary, 17, 31, 83n.8

91

MERIDIAN

Crossing Aesthetics

Peter Szondi, *An Essay on the Tragic*

Peter Fenves, *Arresting Language: From Leibniz to Benjamin*

Jill Robbins, ed., *Is It Righteous to Be?: Interviews with Emmanuel Levinas*

Louis Marin, *Of Representation*

Daniel Payot, *The Architect and the Philosopher*

J. Hillis Miller, *Speech Acts in Literature*

Maurice Blanchot, *Faux pas*

Jean-Luc Nancy, *Being Singular Plural*

Maurice Blanchot / Jacques Derrida, *The Instant of My Death / Demeure: Fiction and Testimony*

Niklas Luhmann, *Art as a Social System*

Emmanual Levinas, *God, Death, and Time*

Ernst Bloch, *The Spirit of Utopia*

Giorgio Agamben, *Potentialities: Collected Essays in Philosophy*

Ellen S. Burt, *Poetry's Appeal: French Nineteenth-Century Lyric and the Political Space*

Jacques Derrida, *Adieu to Emmanuel Levinas*

Werner Hamacher, *Premises: Essays on Philosophy and Literature from Kant to Celan*

Aris Fioretos, *The Gray Book*

Deborah Esch, *In the Event: Reading Journalism, Reading Theory*

Winfried Menninghaus, *In Praise of Nonsense: Kant and Bluebeard*

Giorgio Agamben, *The Man Without Content*

Giorgio Agamben, *The End of the Poem: Studies in Poetics*

Massimo Cacciari, *Posthumous People: Vienna at the Turning Point*

David E. Wellbery, *The Specular Moment: Goethe's Early Lyric and the Beginnings of Romanticism*

Edmond Jabès, *The Little Book of Unsuspected Subversion*

Hans-Jost Frey, *Studies in Poetic Discourse: Mallarmé, Baudelaire, Rimbaud, Hölderlin*

Pierre Bourdieu, *The Rules of Art: Genesis and Structure of the Literary Field*

Nicolas Abraham, *Rhythms: On the Work, Translation, and Psychoanalysis*

Jacques Derrida, *On the Name*

David Wills, *Prosthesis*

Maurice Blanchot, *The Work of Fire*

Jacques Derrida, *Points . . . : Interviews, 1974–1994*

J. Hillis Miller, *Topographies*

Philippe Lacoue-Labarthe, *Musica Ficta (Figures of Wagner)*

Jacques Derrida, *Aporias*

Emmanuel Levinas, *Outside the Subject*

Jean-François Lyotard, *Lessons on the Analytic of the Sublime*

Peter Fenves, *"Chatter": Language and History in Kierkegaard*

Jean-Luc Nancy, *The Experience of Freedom*

Jean-Joseph Goux, *Oedipus, Philosopher*

Haun Saussy, *The Problem of a Chinese Aesthetic*

Jean-Luc Nancy, *The Birth to Presence*

The authorized representative in the EU for product safety and compliance is:
Mare Nostrum Group
B.V Doelen 72
4831 GR Breda
The Netherlands

www.ingramcontent.com/pod-product-compliance
Lightning Source LLC
Chambersburg PA
CBHW031446280326
41927CB00037B/373